THE HURRY-UP, NO-HUDDLE:
An Offensive Philosophy

Gus Malzahn

©2003 Coaches Choice. All rights reserved. Printed in the United States.

No part of this book may be reproduced, stored in a retrieval system or transmitted, in any form or by any means, electronic, mechanical, photocopying, recording, or otherwise, without the prior permission of Coaches Choice.

ISBN: 1-58518-654-6
Library of Congress Control Number: 2002105659
Book layout and diagrams: Deborah Oldenburg
Cover design: Kerry Hartjen

Coaches Choice
P.O. Box 1828
Monterey, CA 93942
www.coacheschoice.com

DEDICATION

This book is dedicated to my Lord and Savior Jesus Christ. He has blessed me unbelievably in my life and has given me the opportunity to do something that I love as my career. Also, this book is to my beautiful wife, Kristi, for her unconditional love and support that she has given me on a consistent basis, no matter what the circumstances. And finally, this book is for my two girls, Kylie and Kenzie, who are the joy of my life.

ACKNOWLEDGMENTS

The old cliché that says you're only as good as the people around you holds true in my life. The Lord has blessed me through my career by putting me in the right place at the right time with coaches and players who were loyal, hardworking, and dedicated to being a champion.

During my eleven-year coaching journey, there have been many people who have made an impact on my life; all are very deserving of recognition. First, I want to thank the coaches who directly impacted the shaping of the Hurry-Up No Huddle philosophy. Chris Wood, who has the sharpest offensive mind of any coach I have ever been around. Greg Hughes who had a huge role in getting the Shiloh program to an elite level, and Kevin Johnson who has been my assistant head coach for the past four years and deserves a lot of credit for our success.

Pastor Ronnie W. Floyd has shown friendship, support, and love of the game of football, which has helped me begin to realize my dreams. I will never be able to repay Phil Phillips for his unwavering support, but mostly for his example of TRUE servant leadership. I would also like to thank Jimmy Dykes for taking a chance by hiring a little known coach from Hughes High School, thereby making it possible for me to coach at Shiloh Christian High School.

This book was compiled with the help of many people, with special thanks going to Mike Reagan, who is an outstanding football coach with a bright future for his many hours of assistance and advice in the writing of this book. Also, thank you to Stacey Grigg, who helped proof the pages of this book.

Finally, a system is only as strong as the players within it. Thank you to the players at Shiloh Christian High School from 1996-2000 and my current players at Springdale High School who have worked extremely hard and believed in a system that is considered different and unusual. Also thank you to all the coaches I have been privileged to work with over the years.

FOREWORD

I met Gus Malzahn in the spring of 1995 while serving as the athletic director at Shiloh Christian High School. I was searching for a coach with the vision to take our football program to the championship level. After a two-hour conversation with him, I hired him, knowing he had all of the qualities I look for in a winner. He had a *passion* for the game of football. He had *discipline* already built into his life that only a very few people understand. He was full of *competitive* fire that could not be disguised for anything other than a person who wanted to win, and win with integrity. I also saw another quality that all great coaches possess at every level. He was very *intelligent* and always looking for an advantage over his opponents.

Passion, discipline, competitive fire, and *intelligence* are what drove Gus Malzahn to come up with a winning formula to produce state championship teams and national-record setters on the offensive side of the football. For the next five years as our head football coach, Gus Malzahn was the potter, and out of the clay, he produced and perfected the nation's best HURRY UP NO HUDDLE offense that the high school level had ever seen.

As a former college basketball player, coach, and now ESPN college analyst, I quickly saw the similarities between his offense and a fast-breaking, high-scoring, basketball team. Conditioning, timing, discipline and attention to detail were all in place. His teams were the aggressor for the entire game! Opponents could not take a possession off or points would be put on the board.

Like anything else in life, you will only reap what you sow. I have personally seen the countless hours of practice, preparation, and sacrifice made by his staff and players. If you study these pages with a sharp mind and pay great attention to the details, you and your team will benefit. However, if you choose to study the offensive system with not only great attention to detail but are also driven with a heart of a champion, only then will you reach the championship and record-setting level. I'm honored to know Gus Malzahn as a coach; he has all of my respect. I am blessed to have him as a friend.

Jimmy Dykes
ESPN Sports Announcer

CONTENTS

Dedication 3

Acknowledgements 4

Foreword 5

Preface 8

Chapter 1: Understanding the Philosophy of the Hurry-Up, No-Huddle .. 11

Chapter 2: Before Implementing the Hurry-Up, No-Huddle 20

**Chapter 3: Building a Well-Organized Offensive System with
the Hurry-Up, No-Huddle** 23

Chapter 4: Hurry-Up, No-Huddle Communication 35

Chapter 5: How to Practice the Hurry-Up, No-Huddle 51

Chapter 6: The Hurry-Up, No-Huddle Running Game 64

Chapter 7: The Hurry-Up, No-Huddle Passing Game 73

Chapter 8: Tips for Running the Hurry-Up, No-Huddle 84

About the Author 88

PREFACE

Most coaches, upon entering their chosen profession, have dreams and aspirations of winning conference and even state championships. Along their coaching journey, they will spend numerous hours going to clinics, talking with successful coaches, and sometimes just dreaming of ways to obtain a winning edge that will give their program an advantage over their opponents.

I was no different than many of these professionals. From day one, I was striving to find the "edge" I needed a way to help my program to win championships. I attended clinics and met with other coaches that had experienced success. The whole time I was trying to find out what they were doing that I was not doing. While this process was very helpful to me in my career, I have also strived to have something unique in my program that was different than other programs around me. I always believed there had to be something out there that I was missing. In 1997, I found that one thing that was different. That is when the "hurry-up no-huddle" was born.

We had just ended the 1996 season and were not too pleased with a 6-win and 6-loss record. My staff and I came together with one goal in mind—finding a way to get our team to the state championship game the following year. Of course, as with all programs, several factors were working against us that would have to be considered. First, we live in the northwest part of Arkansas, which is considered by many individuals in my state to be lacking the caliber of athletes necessary to win state championships. The second factor was a reaffirmation of the first—only one program had won a state championship in any classification in this part of the state in 25 years.

As a result, we knew we had a huge challenge ahead of us. My staff and I also knew we had to design something extreme and different to achieve our goal. We had experimented with starting the game with a no-huddle series of three plays, at a two-minute, "hurry-up" pace, that we had scripted and practiced the previous week. When we did this, we discovered that our team was energized, and the crowd was excited and intrigued. As a consequence, this three-play sequence enabled our team to establish momentum for a relatively short period of time.

However, as soon as the scripted plays were run, we would then go back to huddling up and would inevitably lose our momentum. Needless to say, our thinking was to find a way to keep the momentum and not have to go back to huddling. My offensive coordinator at the time, Chris Wood, was a graduate assistant at Arkansas Tech where they had run some no huddle the year before he arrived at Shiloh. His background provided him the opportunity to bring some experience and good ideas to our search for an answer to our dilemma.

Subsequently, we began brainstorming and toying with the idea of not only running the no huddle, but also the "hurry up" at a two-minute pace for a full four quarters. We began weighing the positives and the negatives. Some of the positives we found were the game would definitely be more exciting, and we could quickly establish momentum in the game. Not only would it be unique but at the least, the defenses at first would never have seen anything like it.

The only negative we could foresee was a rather large one. If it did not work, we could lose our jobs. A few other concerns existed. Would our team be physically able to run the hurry up, no huddle for four quarters? Would we be able to execute our offense successfully at this pace?

After a while, we decided to take a chance and figuratively jump right in with both feet, hoping that this new innovative offensive system would be the "edge" we had been trying to find. Five years later, I can honestly say this was one of the best decisions I have ever made. Not only did going with the hurry up pace of the no-huddle offense give our team a competitive edge, it also helped us reach our goal–playing in a state championship game. In fact, once we adopted the hurry-up, no-huddle offense, we reached the state championship finals four consecutive years. It also helped us become one of the nation's top yardage-producing, high school gridiron teams, averaging almost 7,000 yards of total offense over this period of time. Table P-1 illustrates the dramatic effect that the hurry-up, no-huddle offense had on our offensive stats. It's little wonder that the Hurry-Up, No-Huddle has forever changed the way I look at the game of football. If it has a similar effect on coaches who read this book, then the time to write it will have been well worth the effort.

YEAR	RECORD	POINTS PER GAME	PASSING YARDS	RUSHING YARDS	TOTAL YARDS	TOTAL PLAYS	TD PASS	INT
*1996	6-6	15.5	1440	1587	3027	491	13	9
1997	14-1	30.0	4075	2638	6713	892	45	6
1998	15-0	39.5	5272	2127	7399	870	66	11
1999	15-0	43.6	4699	2297	6996	892	62	14
2000	13-1-1	36.5	4318	1839	6157	816	53	15

Table P-1. Offensive statistics for the Shiloh Christian High School football team during the period 1996-2000.

Before the Hurry-Up, No-Huddle Offense was adopted prior to the 1997 season.

CHAPTER 1

Understanding the Philosophy of the Hurry-Up, No-Huddle

What is the Hurry-Up, No-Huddle?

In my opinion, two different types of "no huddle" philosophies exist. The first one involves getting to the line of scrimmage, seeing how the defense is aligned, and then having enough time to signal in the proper play that has the best chance of being successful. The second philosophy of the no huddle is the two-minute offense that has a fast and furious pace that you would run toward the end of the game when you are behind. The *HURRY UP NO HUDDLE* is just as its title says. It is the second philosophy that I described. The only difference is we run our offense at that fast and furious pace the entire game.

The *HURRY UP NO HUDDLE* philosophy is designed to completely change the dynamics of the traditional game of football. The advantages that you will have are numerous, and if you do not have the talent of your opponents, this can be the great equalizer at any level of football because this philosophy allows the offense to be the aggressor and keep constant pressure on the defense and the defensive coaches. If you want to give your program a boost, to excite your players, coaches, and fans, then this way of thinking is for you. Hopefully, this offense will open your eyes to a completely new way of looking at the game of football.

Game-Related Goals

We have three main goals that we go into each ballgame trying to achieve. Each goal complements the other two. In turn, we feel if we accomplish all three, we will win the game.

- **#1–Speed up the game.**

You can accomplish this goal by snapping the football within five seconds after the referee puts the ball into play. This step can be a challenge if you use a lot of motion in your offense, but it should only cost you a couple of extra seconds. If you can snap the ball at this type of pace, then you will be able to control the tempo and get the defense out of their normal routine. You want to turn the game into a fast break type of football game.

If you have ever watched the pace of an up-tempo basketball game, that is the pace you want to carry over to the football field. While it may sound a little crazy, you can get the same advantages in football as you would if you were controlling the tempo of the basketball game. If you could go back to the first basketball team that ever ran the fast break and could execute it effectively, you know they had to have a huge advantage at first until everyone got used to the speed of the game where they could defend it. The same factor applies in football. The *hurry-up, no-huddle* is equivalent to the fast break. As such, a window of time exists that can give you an unbelievable advantage until more and more teams run it or learn to defend it. While in many quarters, the trend today is to run a no huddle offense, the key difference in this situation is running the no-huddle at a hurry-up pace for the entire game.

- **#2–Lengthen the game.**

Lengthening the game refers to the actual "playing time" of a game, not the time it takes from start to finish. Most high school games involve between seven and eight minutes of actual playing time in a forty-eight minute game. You want to turn the game into a five-quarter football game and increase the actual playing time two to three minutes. It does not sound like much, but it will add an entire quarter of playing time to the game. Most teams talk of winning the fourth quarter. We talk to our kids about getting to and winning the fifth quarter.

As a rule, most coaches, deep down inside, like to be aggressive and take chances. By using the *hurry-up, no-huddle* philosophy, you will be encouraged and allowed to take more chances on offense, defense, and special teams. For example, we use four different onside kicks at any given time during a game. We will also go for it on fourth down sometimes in our own territory. We instill in our players its just another down to get a first down, and we do not panic if we do not get it. If we do punt, we like to quick kick with our quarterback from our regular shotgun formation, so an opposing team cannot set up a return.

You also need to be aggressive on defense. One of your biggest fears would be for a team to hold the ball with long drives and shorten game. The first year that we ran the *hurry-up, no-huddle*, we learned this lesson the hard the way in the 1997 state championship game. We were beaten fifty-four to thirty in a game that our opponents controlled the pace and shortened the game. During that game, we did not blitz much and did not take chances on offense or special teams. As a consequence, we paid the price for our lack of aggressiveness. Fortunately, we learned from our mistakes. Accordingly, we have not been conservative since.

One of the biggest challenges a coach will face when using the *hurry-up, no-huddle* philosophy is that you have to have the mentality that if you get beat, it may be by a lot because you are lengthening the game. We have been in a few games that we were behind three or four touchdowns early in the game. If we had not had this mentality, we would have lost them all. The hardest losses for most coaches are the close ones. Those type games are the ones that tend to stick with you the longest. More often than not, the blowouts seem to be a little bit easier to live with in the long run.

- **#3–Mentally and physically wear down your opponent.**

You can achieve this objective by keeping constant pressure on your opponent. If you achieve the previous two goals, then this goal is usually a given. The key to this particular goal is having your kids in great shape. How you help get your kids in top physical condition will be discussed further in Chapter 3. The best example I could personally give for achieving all three goals would have to be our 1999 quarterfinal playoff game versus Junction City, Arkansas–a contest that ended up in a victory for us by a mind-boggling score of 70-64. It was selected by *Student Sports Magazine* as the

national high school game of the year. The first question that will probably come to your mind is, "just how bad were both defenses." The funny thing about it, is that coming into the game, both teams were undefeated. Junction City was only giving up four points per game, and we were only giving up eleven. It was the wildest experience of my coaching career.

The game statistics were unbelievable:

- The two teams combined for 1454 total yards—794 by Shiloh Christian and 660 by Junction City.

- The teams earned a total of 51 first downs—36 by Shiloh Christian and 15 by Junction City.

- The two teams combined to score 134 points—Shiloh Christian 70 Junction City 64.

- Junction City rushed for 628 yards, led by Marcus Godfrey's 308 yards on 22 carries scoring three touchdowns.

- Shiloh Christians sophomore quarterback Rhett Lashlee passed for 672 yards—then a national record.

- Shiloh Christian had two receivers over the 200-yard reception mark. Cole McNair had 16 catches for 264 yards, and David Meyer had 10 catches for 212 yards.

Shiloh Christian
Quarterback
Rhett Lashlee

QUARTER	SHILOH CHRISTIAN	JUNCTION CITY
1ST	14	38
2ND	35	51
3RD	55	58
4TH	70	64

Table 1-1. Quarter-by-quarter running score of the Shiloh Christian vs. Junction City game.

Game Overview

We knew going into the game that we were facing a very talented and extremely fast team. Our coaches really thought we would need to score fifty points to win, never imagining it would take 70 to win. I should have known that it was going to be a wild night. Before the game, the power was knocked out when a large truck backed into a transformer. It was pitch black for an hour in front of a capacity crowd. The game started an hour and a half late, and the scoreboard didn't work which upset me.

Little did I know however, that the malfunctioning scoreboard would be an advantage for us when we got so far behind early and our kids couldn't see the score.

- **First Quarter**

The first quarter was a complete nightmare. Junction City ran five plays in its first three possessions, and three went the distance for touchdown runs of 39, 93, and 79 yards, respectively. Before we could blink, it was thirty-one to seven, and I recall the public address announcer saying, "Marcus Godfrey (Junction City's star running back) has rushed for 238 yards and three touchdowns on five carries, and there's still two minutes left to go in the first quarter." I looked at my defensive coordinator, Kevin Johnson, and said, "They're going to score a hundred points, and he's going to run for a thousand yards." He looked back at me with a blank expression and agreed. We were past the point of being angry. We were more in a state of shock. At that point, we had to make a choice. Should we throw in the towel and try to get the game over and save some embarrassment, or hang in the battle. At this point in the situation, we had to find out if we truly believed in the hurry-up, no-huddle philosophy. At the end of the first quarter, we were trailing 38 to 14. We then pulled our team to the side and told our players we weren't quitting, and we had to make the game as long as possible. We told our kids to get out of bounds every time possible and we started onside kicking from the second quarter on.

- **Second Quarter**

Despite the fact that the score was 38-14 at the beginning of the second quarter, we were feeling a little better because we saw that at least our offense could move the football on them (even though we hadn't figured out how to stop them yet). We pulled to within sixteen points to make the score 51-35 right before the half. We then recovered an onside kick but ended up throwing an interception in the end zone on the last play of the first half. But as I watched their players leaving the field, I noticed some of their athletes were jogging slowly, while others were walking laboriously to their dressing room. Our guys, on the other hand, sprinted to our locker room. A few moments later, I told our coaches, "We are going to win this game." This was the first time during the game that I had felt that way.

- **Third Quarter**

Beginning the third quarter with the score 51-35, we felt the momentum was going in our favor. Junction City had a lot of pride and character. Even though they were tired, they continued to battle. In this quarter, we finally made them punt, and ended up scoring three times to their one. By the time the quarter had ended, we had closed the gap to three points, with Junction City still ahead 58-55.

- Fourth Quarter

The fourth quarter was stressful to say the least. We managed to trade scores, but still found ourselves behind with four minutes remaining on our own ten-yard line. We then went on a 90-yard drive that ended with a touchdown pass that gave us the lead for the first and only time of the game with two minutes left. Subsequently, we held them on downs and won the game 70 to 64.

- Post Game

When the game was over, the result was like a dream. To go from worrying about getting embarrassed to winning the game was unbelievable. It was a shame someone had to lose this game. Quite obviously, if we had not had the hurry-up, no-huddle that night, we wouldn't have won the game or the state championship that year. This goes to show that the old saying that, "defense wins championships" is not always true.

This game was a perfect example of accomplishing the three goals we have for every game. Our first goal was to speed up the game. This goal was definitely accomplished by the fast pace of the scoring in the game, even though we were behind. Our second goal of lengthening the game and getting to the fifth quarter was achieved not only by the total number of plays being 149, but also by onside kicking after every score, and going for it on fourth down on every series after the first quarter. The third goal of mentally and physically wearing down our opponents can best be shown by looking at the quarter-by-quarter scoring summary. Table 1-2 illustrates just how our opponents wore down. Junction City suffered a gradual decline in their scoring in each quarter, while our level of scoring remained the same. The fact Junction City only scored seven points in the third quarter and six in the fourth indicates how tired they really got.

QUARTER	JUNCTION CITY	SHILOH CHRISTIAN
1ST	38	14
2ND	13	21
3RD	7	20
4TH	6	15

Table 1-2. Quarter-by-quarter scoring summary for the Shiloh Christian vs. Junction City game.

Advantages of the Hurry-Up, No-Huddle

Every coach is always looking for a competitive advantage. The hurry-up, no huddle can provide you and your team with numerous advantages, including the following:

- You will set the tempo of the game

By running your offense at such a fast pace, it will allow you to set the tempo of the game and establish the momentum in your favor. When you think of tempo and momentum, you naturally think of a basketball game. Utilizing the **hurry-up, no-huddle** enables the same situation to occur during the football game. And when you are setting the tempo, you have a great advantage because defenses are not used to the pace set by the hurry-up, no-huddle.

- **Gives the coach the ability to change the play at the line of scrimmage after he sees the defensive alignment**

If for no other reason to run the no huddle, having the capability to change the play after you've seen the defensive alignment is more justification to adopt this offense. How many coaches have ever called a play that they knew wouldn't work before the snap of the ball because of the defensive alignment. In essence, the hurry-up, no huddle has solved this problem. For example, on an important fourth-down play, you've called an outside power, and the defense has loaded up on that side. Most coaches have to run the play or call time out. Teams that employ the hurry-up, no-huddle do not have to run another play that would otherwise be stopped because of a defensive alignment. If you get stopped now, it is due to a breakdown or the defense has physically whipped you. The hurry-up, no-huddle gives you the ability to change the play at the line of scrimmage, thereby giving your team the best chance of being successful.

- It is fun for players and fans

If your program needs a boost, the hurry-up, no-huddle can provide it. You will find that your kids tend to work harder and take pride in doing something different and unique, especially after seeing the benefits from the game situations. This style of football intrigues not only the hardcore but also the individuals who are not normally football fans. At Shiloh Christian, football enthusiasts, attendance has increased every year for the past five years. For example, our 2001 regular season game against the Springdale Bulldogs, over 25,000 fans were in the stands–a total that almost doubled the previous record attendance for a high school football game in the state of Arkansas. The unique aspect of the game is that both teams ran the hurry-up, no huddle.

- You'll get more kids out to play

The hurry-up, no-huddle tends to get more kids out to play this style of football then normally would play football. Because many kids have so many extracurricular activities to choose from today, the hurry-up, no-huddle makes going out for football more fun and attractive than it otherwise might be in order to get the good athletes out of the hallways and onto the field. For example this past season, one of our school's better track/basketball athletes–an individual who had never played football before–came out and played wide receiver. He ended up making all-conference and earning a college scholarship. If you were to ask him, he would tell you he would have never came out if it weren't for the exciting brand of football involved with the hurry-up, no-huddle.

- **Score points quickly**

Scoring points quickly can get your opponents out of their game plan early. Since implementing the hurry up five years ago, our teams have averaged 33 points in the first half. Due to this, teams which normally would be considered "running teams" have to attempt to keep up by throwing the ball. During this period, our average scoring drive has been 61 yards on six plays, taking 1 minute 23 seconds. Not surprisingly, this situation is demoralizing to our opponents.

- **It gives you more offensive snaps**

The number of offensive snaps is the most important stat with which you should be concerned. You should not worry about time of possession, only the number of plays. Prior to our 1996 season, we were a ball-control team that would milk the clock and shorten the game. We averaged approximately 41 snaps a game. Once we implemented the hurry-up, no-huddle, we averaged over 60 plays a game, even though we often were running out the clock in the fourth quarter in most of our games. The highest number of plays we've had in a game was 96 in a 47-46 non-overtime win–a total that almost set a national record. In that game, our junior quarterback, Rhett Lashlee, attempted 72 passes, again almost setting a national record.

- **Defenses cannot simulate it in practice**

In one-week's time, teams cannot simulate the speed and efficiency that they will see on Friday night from teams that are employing the hurry-up, no-huddle. In that regard, opposing coaches who have faces us have stated that even when using two scout teams, they were still unable to match the pace of the game.

- **Defenses have to spend more time than usual preparing for us**

Defenses not only have to prepare for your offensive scheme, they also have to prepare for the hurry-up, no-huddle aspect separately. This factor takes away from their time to focus on your offensive plays. Teaching their athletes to line up quickly and correctly can be a major task. It can be an even bigger challenge if the defenses are trying to match up personnel.

- **Stops defenses from regrouping after big plays**

Most defensive coordinators have the goal of regrouping after a play of 25 yards or more. The hurry-up, no-huddle enables you can keep defenses on their heels after big plays, and not allow them to get in the huddle to motivate each other. If they want to stop your momentum, they have to call time out.

- **Makes it harder to pick up tendencies**

Most offensive teams have a lot of tendencies in their offense. If you run the hurry-up, no-huddle, you don't have to worry about the other team picking up your tendencies, because you know how hard it is for your defensive players, even in a slow-placed practice setting, to call out the main plays according to our scout team's formation. As a result, the defenses will face a unique challenge when attempting to respond to the pace established by the hurry-up, no-huddle. Defenses have to worry about lining up properly first, before they can think about the play that may be dictated by the formation or the situation.

- **Creates problems for defensive coaches**

The hurry-up, no-huddle enables you to get an opponent's defensive coordinator out of his normal routine. He is used to analyzing the situation according to down-and-distance. In the traditional approach, a defensive coordinator then looks at an offense's tendencies, figures out what to call, and signals the defensive call to the huddle within 25 seconds. The hurry-up, no-huddle gets him out of this comfort zone and forces him to make quick decisions. No need exists for you to be smarter than anyone else. On the other hand, because you have practiced and are used to having to think quickly, you can almost always make better decisions than your opponent at the accelerated pace.

- **Finding ways to communicate to their defenses**

In a regular game, players are used to huddling up. In the huddle, one designated player looks at the coach for a signal, and then relays it to the other players who are getting a 25-second rest. In the hurry up, the defensive coordinator will have to be creative to signal his calls to all eleven players. Even if only one player does not get the correct call, then the hurry up is definitely worth the effort. Most of the opposing coaches have used numbers, colors, or combinations of both to try to achieve this. Although we are not in the signal stealing business, we usually have a good idea of an opponent's defense before the play by the third or fourth series of a game.

CHAPTER 2

Before Implementing the Hurry-Up, No-Huddle

Before deciding whether to adopt the *hurry-up, no-huddle* style of play, you should consider the following six points:

- **You need to be an average or better offensive football team.**

If you have a below-average football team, the hurry-up, no-huddle may be a bigger challenge for you to implement and succeed at. However, you do not have to be a great offensive team to make it work. For example, during my first year at Springdale High School, we were an average football team. But by implementing the hurry-up, it enabled us to lead our conference (AAAAA West), which is considered the top conference in the state, in total offensive yards, passing yards, scoring, and we ended up breaking 12 school records at a school that had been traditionally one of the top programs in the state.

The reason I say we were an average offensive team was that we had one offensive starter back from the previous year, who was an offensive lineman that moved from center to guard. Our quarterback had never taken a varsity snap and our two leading receivers included a player who had been a kicker is entire life, and the other had never played football before and did not even know how to put on his equipment properly—and he ended up being one of our go-to guys. As long as you happen to be an average or better football team, then this system is definitely for you. You will set yourself apart from your opponents in a *hurry*. Running the hurry-up will give you more opportunities to clinch the game early in the first half, even against quality opponents.

- **You cannot worry about your total time of possession.**

Many coaches have a problem believing this because in a traditional ball-control, field-position, defensive game, the team that wins the total time of possession usually has a good chance of winning. You should not care about time of possession. The only thing you should care about is the number of snaps and the score.

We average around 15 minutes in time of possession in a 48-minute game. Figure 2-1 highlights the total time of possession for us and our opponents, and the final scores in our four state championship games.

1997	54-30 Loss	Opponent	34:32	Us	13.28
1998	49-14 Win	Opponent	32:33	Us	15:27
1999	47-35 Win	Opponent	33:47	Us	14:13
2000	30-29 Loss	Opponent	31:29	Us	16:31

Figure 2-1

As you can see, the chart illustrates that the extremely low time of possession really means nothing as far as winning or losing a game. To further illustrate this, in a 1998 regular season game, we had the ball for only 8 minutes and 22 seconds and were able to win the game 42 to 21. Of course this is an extreme example, but it also adds validity to the fact that time of possession is irrelevant when running the hurry-up, no-huddle.

- **You cannot worry about your defensive statistics.**

When considering the hurry-up, no huddle offensive system, many head coaches are worried that their defensive coordinators will no *buy* into the philosophy. Most defensive coordinators take pride in their defensive statistics and feel that these numbers will eventually help them move up in the coaching profession. Just remind them that only their defensive goals need to be adjusted—the offense will take care of the rest.

- **Your players must be in great physical condition.**

At first, when you let your athletes know how much conditioning is involved in the hurry-up, they will all look at you as if you've lost your mind. But after the first time they see how advantageous it is to be in top physical condition implementing this system in an actual game, they will be sold on it forever. Your athletes will go from dreading it and just trying to survive it, to getting excited about it and challenging one another in practice. You should set up your practices keeping rest time at a minimum. (This will be illustrated in more detail in Chapter 5).

You should also condition your athletes at the end of each practice, and always run the same amount from week one through your last game. Remember, if a track runner ever lets up on conditioning during his season, he will be at a disadvantage facing his opponents. The same is true for your athletes.

- **Your offensive staff has to be prepared to make quick decisions.**

This can be one of the bigger challenges at first, because you and your offensive staff will need practice at *thinking quick* just like your players. After a short adjustment period, you and your staff will get used to the pace. Eventually you will be amazed that you ever took a full 25 seconds to call a play, but you must know your offensive system inside and out. A communication system that will help you make these quicker decisions will be discussed in more detail in Chapter 4. When you call a play during a game, your next play needs to be ready before the ball is snapped. Again, this may seem difficult at first, but it's like anything else you do on your team—the more you practice it, the better you get.

- **You have to be committed to the philosophy.**

Some coaches, after the first time they faced a little adversity using the hurry-up, no-huddle philosophy, go back to their old ball-control offensive philosophy. Remember, it won't go smoothly at first and you will experience some *growing* pains, but if you keep practicing and perfecting the system, it will take your program to a level that you could only dream of before. You need to believe in what you and your team are trying to accomplish.

CHAPTER 3

Building a Well-Organized Offensive System with the Hurry-Up, No-Huddle

With every successful team you will find a well-organized offensive system. To be successful at running the hurry-up, no-huddle, it is no different and even more of an important factor. The offense is moving at such a fast pace that it not only has to be able to work quickly, but it also has to be simple enough to understand. If you feel good about your current system and have had success with it, then you may not need to make any changes other than adapting the principles of the hurry-up philosophy. If you have doubts about your current offensive system, then you should ask yourself the following four questions about your offense's ability to run the hurry-up, no-huddle.

- Do you have an offensive scheme that enables you to execute successful plays against any defensive formation?
- Is your current offensive system simple, consistent, and easy for players and coaches to learn and understand?
- Do you have rules within your current system allowing your players to recognize an unsuccessful play?
- Do you have the ability to change the play at the line of scrimmage after you recognize the possibility of an unsuccessful play?

If you cannot say yes to all four questions, you should consider modifying your offensive system to incorporate the hurry-up philosophy.

It's important to note that any style of offense, whether it be *wide-open, option-oriented, Wing-T,* or *run-and-shoot,* can adopt the hurry-up philosophy and be successful at it. The wide-open offense is the system that we use. This type of offense is a good example of a simple and systematic approach.

Formations

You can run numerous plays using only three base formations in the wide-open offense. You should teach your players to recognize defensive alignments, coverages, and the defensive player responsibilities based on these formations. Using only three formations will allow your players to learn and apply the wide-open offense with minimal confusion. Many teams have many different formations and run only a few plays from all of them. This way of thinking can be just as successful, but using only three base formations will be easier for your coaches and players to execute this type of offense quickly and efficiently.

The three base formations are based on the number of running backs in the backfield. The *trips* formation is the no-back or empty formation. The *doubles* formation is the one-back formation, and the *pro* formation is the standard tight end, flanker, and split end formation with two running backs in the backfield (Figure 3-1, a-c).

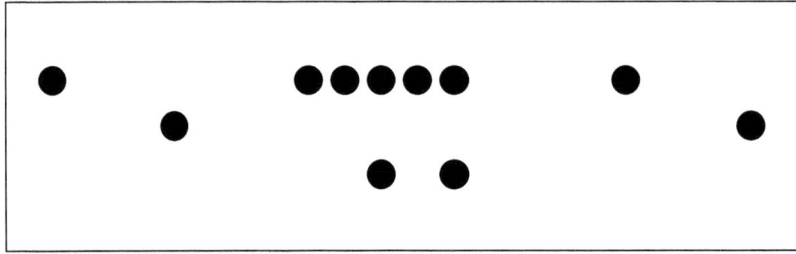

Figure 3-1a: Base Formation—"Doubles"

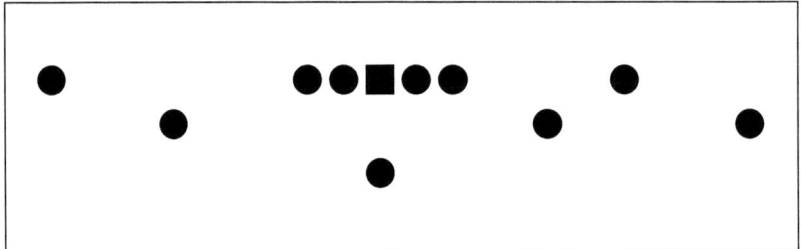

Figure 3-1b: Base Formation—"Trips"

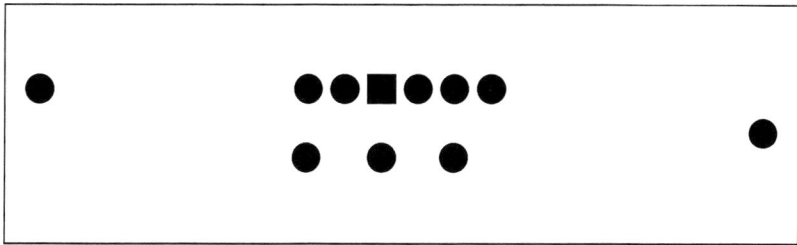

Figure 3-1c: Base Formation–"Pro"

Personnel

You should use a numbering system for your skill-position players when identifying personnel in formations. For example, your quarterback should be labeled number 1 and aligns under the center or four-yards deep in the shotgun. Your flanker should be labeled number 2. He will always be an outside receiver in all formations. Your fullback should be number 3. He will be in the backfield with the quarterback in all formations except for your *empty look*, which is usually called *trips*. The tailback should be labeled number 4 and will align as an inside receiver when split, or in the backfield with the quarterback. Your split end should be labeled number 5. He will align as an outside receiver in all formations. Finally, your tight end should be labeled number 9. He will be an inside receiver in all formations (Figure 3-2, a-c).

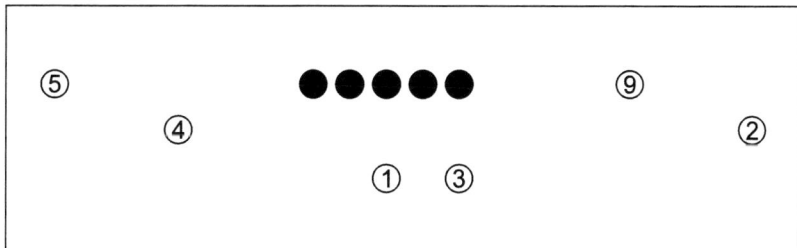

Figure 3-2a: Base Formation–"Doubles"

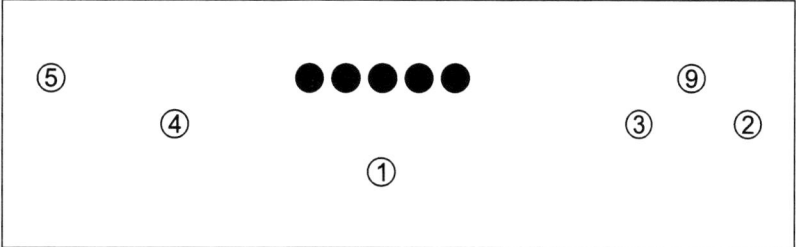

Figure 3-2b: Base Formation–"Trips"

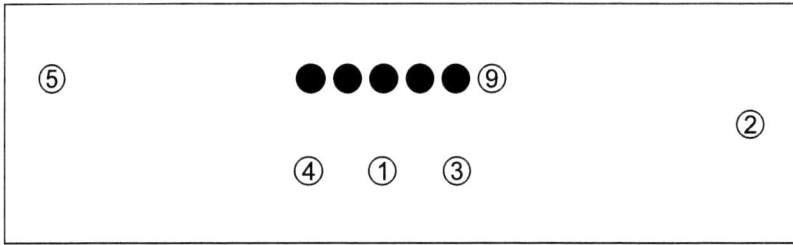

Figure 3-2c: Base Formation—"Pro"

Route Tree

You should use a route tree that gives you the ability to change pass plays quickly and easily. You can do this with the simple procedure of giving the skill-position number and then adding the specific route number that you want the player to run. This will be especially helpful when you or one of your coaches sees a route open up that is not in the normal progression of your quarterback's reads. A route tree gives you the ability to call that play and add to it the adjustment that you saw open up. For example, you would call the same play, but you would tell the quarterback to look for the 5 man on an 8 route instead. A route tree provides a simple and consistent reference guide for your coaches and players to use to make adjustments against the defenses you will face (Figure 3-3).

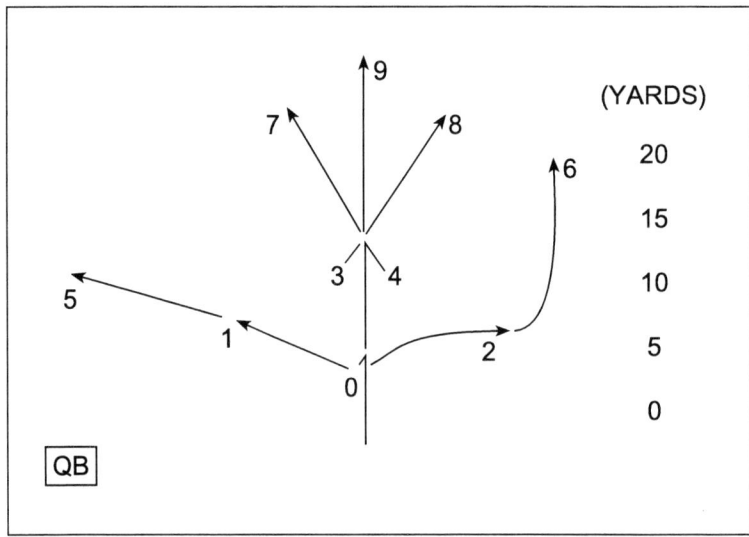

Figure 3-3: Route Tree

Cadence

In the hurry-up system, you should only use a one-snap count. This helps keep the game going at a faster pace and will not allow the defense any rest. The hurry-up needs to have a rhythm to it, so your players can anticipate the snap to get off the ball quicker. The defense will eventually pick up on the snap count, but this can be seen as an advantage. During every third or fourth play, you should call a *dummy/dummy* play to keep the defense honest. You can usually get even well-disciplined teams to jump offsides with these a few times throughout a game. Even if they do not jump offsides, it will slow them down and allow you to recognize their stunts or blitzes on that play (Figure 3-4).

You could use the verbal command of *Jerry* to relay the dummy/dummy play to the players. A good word association to help them memorize this is the Jerry Springer Show.

Figure 3-4

The cadence you should use is very simple. It is made up of a three-word rhythmic call. The first two words indicate the side we are running to. The last word is when the ball is snapped. You could use *Roger* to represent right, and *Liz* to represent left. The reason you should reinforce direction in the cadence is that the names of your plays should not have a direction. These terms will tell your players the direction of the play. For example, your quarterback might say, "Roger—Roger—Hut," or "Liz–Liz–Hut." You can use different words for the directions in your offense if you want to.

But how do you keep the defense from catching on to any of this?

It is simple, because when you call a pass play, you will use the same cadence, "Roger–Roger Hut," and it means absolutely nothing.

Audibles

Using audibles is one of the major advantages to the hurry-up, no-huddle system. You can change the play at the line of scrimmage, allowing you to adjust to the defensive alignment. This system allows your quarterback to change the play quickly, and your offensive players are ready for it. The following are three different ways to audible in the hurry-up.

- Quarterback change

First, the quarterback will have a *rule system* for knowing whether he needs to change the play or not. (This will be discussed later in this chapter.) He will give his offensive teammates a *color* indicating a change in the play. For example, the code color could be *orange*, so whenever the quarterback says *orange*, the offensive players know the play is going to be changed.

- Check with me

This is done after a *dummy/dummy* call. The quarterback will look to the sidelines if the defense does not jump offsides, and wait on the coach to call the next play. This can also be an advantage to the play caller. It gives him a chance to look at the defense before calling the next play. It can be especially effective if he is having trouble recognizing pre-snap defensive coverages. This will allow him to see exactly what the defense is going to do. After receiving the play, the quarterback will give his *orange* call and then the new play.

- Coaches change

If the quarterback does not see that he needs to make a change, then the play caller will yell out the quarterback's first name. This needs to be done *before* the quarterback gets into his cadence. If the play caller does not have a loud enough voice, then another offensive coach with a loud voice should do this job.

Running Game

One of the keys to a successful running game is having a *system of rules* concerning defensive front alignments and the number of defenders in the box. The system also needs to be flexible enough to include all skill-position players to be able to run the ball and not change the linemen's blocking assignments.

We have a total of ten plays in our running system; however, we only run four of these plays on a regular basis. The reason is that we want to effectively execute these four plays against any defensive alignment that we may see. The four plays are the *trap, counter, power,* and *sweep*. Chapter 6 describes these plays in detail.

Ten Running Plays

- Trap
- Counter
- Power
- Sweep
- Blast
- Draw
- Dive
- Dive Option
- Veer
- Veer Option

Running-Game Rules

The following are three major rules you should apply to your running game.

- You should always check the number of defensive players in the box.

This allows you to see if it is conducive to run a successful running play. Use a common sense approach to this; if too many players are in the box to block, then you should change to a pass play.

- Each running play needs a rule that the quarterback can use in determining the side that has the favorable numbers and angles for a successful play.

We will use our trap play as an example here. The rule is when we run the trap, the quarterback will check the 3-technique side or the widest defensive tackle. We expect our linemen and backs to also understand this rule to help us better execute the play (Figure 3-5).

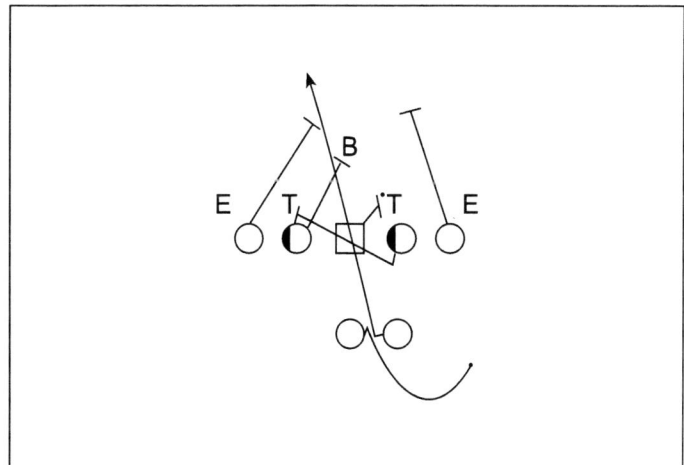

Figure 3-5: Trap. Example: QB Check Trap to 3 Tech. Side.

- Your system must have the flexibility to allow all four backs the opportunity to run any of your base plays without changing your linemen's responsibility.

Using the trap as your example, you have the ability to determine the runner of the trap by adding his personnel number after the trap is called. If you want the quarterback to run the trap, you would put the number 1 after the call, i.e., *Roman 1*. If you want the tailback to run the trap, put the number 4 after the call, i.e., *Roman 4*.

Passing Game

Even though we technically have 33 pass plays total, we only use eight base-combination routes that can run to either side of the field on a regular basis. We want to be able to execute these eight plays to perfection regardless of the defensive coverage on the field. See Chapter 7 for a detailed explanation of passing plays.

Passing-Game Rules

Your coaches and quarterbacks can use the hurry-up system to determine the base-pass plays according to the defensive coverages that they see. The *coverage rules* are broken down into the following three major categories:

- Cover 3 rules
- Cover 2 and 4 rules
- Man-to-Man rules

Cover 3 is a three-deep look with the field divided into thirds. Cover 2 and 4 are similar in the fact that they have a two-safety look, with the difference being the safeties will have half of the field each when playing cover 2. In cover 4, the field is divided into fourths, and each secondary person is responsible for one-fourth of the field. Three types of man-to-man coverages are man-free, two-man, zero-man coverage. Man-free indicates a man under with one safety in the field. Two-man is man under with two safeties deep, and zero-man is man under with no safeties deep. Even though there can be a few variations of the *coverage rules*, you should identify coverages into these three major categories.

We have three to four specific plays within the hurry-up system we use to attack each one of these coverages. For example, if we recognize cover 3, one of the plays we will attack this coverage with is a 4 vertical route. Whereas, if it were a version of man-to-man, we would call some type of crossing route. When using this type of system, it is key for your quarterback and coaches to recognize the pre-snap coverage and to call a play that will be effective against it. How will your quarterback know what play to audible without looking to the sideline for help? It will actually be a very easy job for him because of this *coverage-rules system*.

One of the practice techniques that can help your players recognize different coverages is to go over one of the three base coverages on each practice day. For example, on Mondays you should work on cover 3 plays in the outside period. On Tuesdays, you should work on cover 2/4 plays during outside period, and on Wednesdays, you should work on man-to-man plays. This approach will help you tremendously and will get you feeling comfortable with your passing game against any defensive coverage you will face.

Key Points in Your Passing Game

The ultimate goal for your passing game is to perfect your base-combination routes. You should give your quarterback one defensive player to read and only two receiver options based on that defensive player's actions. If the defense has these two receivers covered, then you should teach your quarterback not to force the ball to the receiver, but to throw the ball away and go on to the next play. Based on four years of statistics, we know this has helped our touchdown-to-interception ratio since using this simplistic approach (Figure 3-6).

YEAR	ATTEMPTS	COMPLETIONS	COMP%	TD	INT
1997	403	243	60.2	45	6
1998	502	295	58.7	66	11
1999	427	249	58.3	62	14
2000	546	305	55.8	54	15

Figure 3-6

Figure 3-7

Even though you should only give your quarterback two options on most plays, if you've called the correct play according to the coverage, you should still be successful. You should have very few route adjustments after the ball is snapped. You want your quarterback to know exactly where the receiver should be. This cuts down on miscommunication and eliminates the statement, "I thought …"

Our quarterbacks and receivers run our base-eight pass-combination routes three days a week during the off-season and summer. This helps them retain our passing game, so they know the timing of the pass routes and can run them with their eyes closed if they had to.

The Play-Calling Board

Using a play-calling board on the field is an important tool for successful teams. It can be made up of one set of colors and three sets of numbers that are 12-inches high. The numbers should be big enough to be seen from across the field (Figure 3-8).

Figure 3-8

The Colors

The first column on the board is made up of five different colors that you can use in your offense: blue, yellow, black, green, and red. Each color determines what to key on the board itself, or the signaler from whom the player gets the proper play. The good thing about using five different colors is your ability to change the color key from week to week, or even change it at half time if you feel the defense is picking up on the color-coding.

Numbering System

You should call your pass plays with a three-number system on your play-calling board.

First Number—*The Series Number*

The first number represents the series number that will define if it is a three-step, five-step, or seven-step drop, and to what side of the field you will be throwing the ball. This number also tells the linemen the depth of where the quarterback will be setting up to throw.

- 4 and 5 is the three-step quick-passing game, 4 being to the right, and 5 to the left.
- 6 and 7 is the five-step passing game, 6 being to the right, and 7 to the left.
- 8 and 9 is the seven-step passing game, 8 being to the right, and 9 to the left.

Second Number—*The Primary Receiver*

The second number identifies who the primary receiver will be by using his personnel number. This also instructs the other receivers what their complementing routes are.

Third Number—*The Route of Primary Receiver*

The third number instructs the primary receiver which route, according to the *route tree*, he will be running. This also instructs the other receivers what their complementing routes are based on the primary receiver's route.

For example, if the play-calling board reads *8-2-0*, then this instructs the quarterback to do a *seven-step drop* looking to the right for the 2 receiver (flanker) to run a *0*, also known as a stop route. This information tells your 9 receiver (tight end) to run an 8 route (flag) over the top of the 2 receiver. This route is commonly known in coaching circles as the *smash* (Figure 3-9).

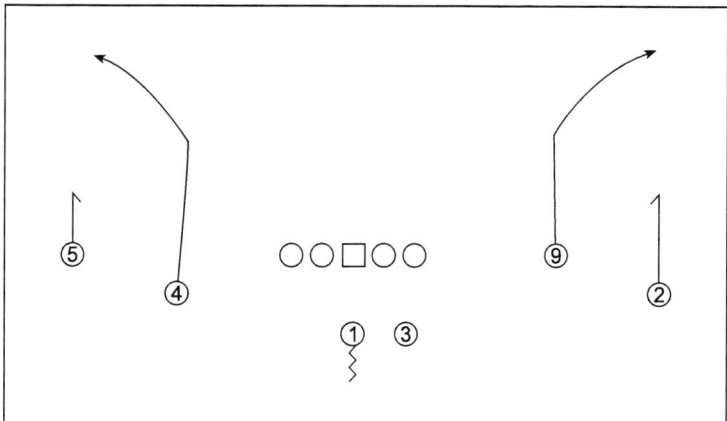

Figure 3-9: Example of 8-2-0.

Another example is if the play-calling board read *4-9-2*. This instructs the quarterback to take a *three-step drop* looking to the right for the *9* receiver (tight end) running a 2 route (out). This information tells your 2 receiver (flanker) to run a 1 route (quick slant) (Figure 3-10).

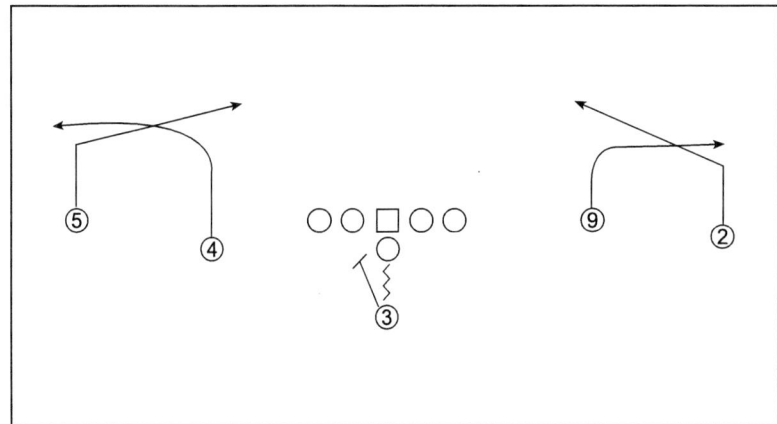

Figure 3-10: Example of 4-9-2.

The color and number play-calling board system is a foolproof way of signaling your plays to your players. We have had numerous coaches attempt to figure out our board over the years. We know of one team who scouted us for five consecutive weeks, their only goal being to figure out how our board worked. Two weeks later we scored 56 points on them. This goes to show the system is unbreakable.

CHAPTER 4

Hurry-Up, No-Huddle Communication

Progression Steps of Communication

The single most important aspect of running the hurry-up, no-huddle effectively is communication. Being able to communicate the desired play to your athletes in a concise, easily understood, and time efficient manner is vital to your team's success. This is one of the major attributes that separates the hurry-up, no-huddle offenses from the time consuming huddle offenses. Clear communication is the ability that allows hurry-up teams to take advantage of defensive coordinators, base defenses, and the clock.

When adapting your offense to the hurry-up pace, you must take into consideration the type of communication system used to relay the play to your athletes. The following are three basic communication systems used by most coaching staffs today.

The first one is to pass it *verbally* from the coach to the player and then on to the huddle. The second is to use *physical movements*, which indicate the desired play and are interpreted by your quarterback. The third is to use a written version, usually in the form of numbers or colors on charts or wristbands that represent the selected play. You can also utilize any combination of the previously mentioned styles.

Coaches need to remember that some people in this profession will go to great lengths to learn the method of relaying plays of their upcoming opponents. With this in mind, the choice of the communication system must be complex enough to hinder opposing coaches, and yet simple enough not to confuse your athletes.

You might find that the verbal method from coach to player is not conducive to the pace you want to play. Also, the opportunity for miscommunication presents itself due to the loudness of the stadium or the player misstating what the coach had told him. Therefore, you might want to use a combination of physical signals and a color/ numbers play-calling board, with a coach in charge of each one. Your quarterback will then relay the necessary information from the coaches to his teammates on the field.

Three basic components that every communication system must relay to the athletes on the field are the *formation, play,* and any *pre-snap motion*. The play caller will give the formation to the signaler for relay to the quarterback. The quarterback will in turn verbally put the offensive team in the proper formation.

For example, your signaling coach will motion in the formation, *doubles right*. *Doubles* is our one-back formation and *right* is the strength of the formation. Without huddling, your offensive team will hustle to the line of scrimmage from the previous play, and the quarterback verbally repeats, "Doubles right," two or three times.

Coaching Point:

- When signaling the strength of formation, instead of holding up the left or right hands, you should always motion to your sideline or the opposite sideline for left and right. This will cut down on the quarterback being confused with left and right, especially when you change directions on the field (Figures 4-1 and 4-2).

Figure 4-1   Figure 4-2

At this point, the quarterback looks at the coach at the color/numbers play-calling board. Colors on the board indicate if the signal coach is *hot* for the play, or if the numbered board is going to be used for this play. For example, the color green might indicate to your players to look at your signaler for the play, while all other colors would key the board.

Being a private Christian school, our plays were designed with the names of Bible characters. Our quarterback would look at the appropriate coach. If it is the signaling coach, then he is signaling in a Bible characters name (*Moses*) and then our quarterback verbally repeats the play two or three times for his teammates. If the board is to be used, the signaling coach then calls out a name that is not a Bible character (*Bob*). This will key the rest of the team to look at the play-calling board to receive the play. By having the quarterback call out the play takes pressure off the rest of the offensive team and will cut down on miscommunication.

Coaching Points:

- You should make sure all skill positions look over to the sideline on every play, and not just the pass plays. This will keep the defense from picking up any tendency for a run play or a pass.

Offensive linemen do not need to look to the sideline. They just need to listen for the quarterback to say the appropriate running play, or if he says a name other than a Bible character, then they would know it is a pass and should listen for the fullback to call out a pass protection. It does not have to be the fullback; it can be the tailback. We use our fullback more in our blocking schemes; therefore, he is in the backfield more often than the tailback. Once again, to avoid having the defense pick up any tendencies based on the verbal calls, make sure the fullback makes pass-protection calls on every play.

The last component to signal is any motion that will be used during the play. The quarterback will verbally yell this one out. Remember, if your offense does not have to use a lot of motion, it can help in saving time, not only in the signaling aspect, but also the snapping of the ball within the five-second window after the official puts the ball into play.

This system of having your quarterback announce all the plays to his teammates is a very safe and efficient way of communicating and is the easiest way to start out. If after a period of time you feel the offensive team can handle not communicating everything through the quarterback, then another successful communication system you can use is based on a *code word*. The code word is the only verbal command to let the offensive players know whether or not to look at the signaler or the play-calling board. In this system, each offensive skill-position player will have to look to the sideline for the play. The only lineman who will look is the tackle closest to the coaches. After he gets the play he will verbally relay it to the rest of the linemen. By only using this tackle allows the rest of your linemen to get set on the ball more quickly and does not slow down the pace of the game. This communication system is best used in a game where noise will probably be factor.

Name of Plays

The first step you should take after deciding to go with the hurry-up is to figure out if your current system of calling plays can be adapted to the hurry-up philosophy. Ask yourself the following three questions:

- Will you be able to call all of your plays from the sideline?
- Will you be able to audible any play into your offense at a quick pace?
- Can you make these calls without giving the defense any indication of what play is about to be executed?

In the hurry-up system, you want to divide your running and passing plays into two categories. One category should be relayed in with numbers and another category should be signaled in with hand or body motions. This will be tougher for defenses to decode and easier for your coaches to communicate with your players. When starting a new naming system for your offensive plays, use the following steps:

- List all of your offensive plays up on a board.
- Separate your running plays from your passing plays and group play-action passes with your running plays.
- Decide on a *theme* for the verbal calling of your plays and audibles.

Meet with your offensive staff and have them write down every offensive play in your playbook. This will give you an idea of how many total plays you are dealing with. Then write all of your running plays and play-action passes on one side of the board, and all of your passing plays on the other.

The reason you should combine your running plays with your play-action plays is because giving names to running plays is easier when you choose a complementing verbal command to help the players recall the play. It also helps your players remember the actual running play they were faking during the play-action pass.

Running Game

Like most football programs, you probably use numbers to call all of your offensive plays. In our old offensive system, the backs were numbered 1 through 4, and the holes for the runner were numbered odd to the left—1 through 9, and even to the right—2 through 8. For example, the running play verbally called *46-power* was designed with the first number being the back, and the second number being the hole on the line. In this case, the 4 back, our tailback, was to go through the 6 hole, off-tackle. The *power* call told every one in the huddle that the fullback would be a lead blocker. We felt that most defenses were familiar with this play-naming technique, and therefore, they would be able to pick up this tendency if we used it to audible at the line of scrimmage. They could then predict the side of the play, overload that side of the line of scrimmage, and make our play unsuccessful. Consequently, we decided to change our numbered running plays to names.

Passing Game

We had a total of 33 passing plays after including the play-action passes with the running game, and subtracting our screens. Our play-calling system was made up of three numbers with the first number being the series, the second number being the primary receiver, and the third number being the route. By giving these three numbers, the rest of our receivers would know their assignments. It would've been an easy decision for us to keep the naming of our passing game the same, but we still changed to names for all our plays.

Choosing a Theme

After deciding to use names, you should choose a *theme* for your plays and audibles. The following are several things to consider when choosing the subject for your theme:

- The theme needs to be simple for the players to remember and relate to. It should not be too detailed or confusing.
- The theme needs to be taught with a *word association* that is easy for your players to understand and remember. The best way for your players to memorize and then recall your system is for them to be able to associate the theme with another idea.
- The theme needs to be consistent throughout the entire system. Therefore, it needs to be *broad* enough to encompass all of your plays.
- The theme needs to have some relationships within itself in order for play-action passes to complement the running plays.
- The theme must allow the verbal commands to be interpreted with physical motions by the signaler.
- The theme must be flexible enough to expand in the future if necessary.

While brainstorming for the theme, keep in mind that every idea is a *good* idea. Even though some ideas may seem odd at first, they may be great ideas down the road.

As mentioned earlier, we were at a Christian school, and we decided to use Bible names as our theme. After all, our kids were already familiar with the Bible and the stories that went with the characters. The following is a list of our running plays with their complementing play-action passes based on Biblical characters (Figure 4-3).

Old Running Play Name	New Name	Old Play-Action Pass Name	New Name
46-47 Power	Moses	46-47 Power Pass	Egypt
Association: Moses led God's people out of Egypt.			
42-43 Blast	Daniel	42-43 Blast Pass	Lion
Association: Daniel was put in the Lion's den.			
44-45 Counter	David	44-45 Waggle Pass	Giant
Association: David killed the Giant.			
32-33 Dive	John	32-33 Option 32-33 Option Pass	Baptist Behead
Association: John was the first to Baptize and was eventually Beheaded.			
34-35 Veer	Noah	34-35 Veer Option	Ark
Association: Noah built the Ark.			
48-49 Sweep	Peter	48-49 Sweep Pass	Water
Association: Peter walked on the Water.			
10-11 Draw	Joshua	30-31 Trap	Roman

Figure 4-3

By looking at the chart, you can see the association technique that we used. We related each football play to a major Biblical character, and the complementing play-action pass with a key aspect in the character's Bible. This greatly increased our players' memory retention. For example, the *44-45 counter* was changed to *David*. Its play-action complement, the *44-45 waggle pass*, was changed to *Giant* because our players knew the story of *David* killing the *Giant*.

Another example, the *32-33 dive*, was changed to the name of *John*. Its running play complement, the *32-33 dive option*, was changed to the name *Baptist*, and its play-action pass complement, the *32-33 Option Pass*, was changed to *Behead* because our players knew the story of *John the Baptist* who was the first to *baptize*, and who was eventually *beheaded*. This theme association technique helped our players recall the play progression easily and efficiently.

We chose the Bible as our theme, but many other possible theme choices are available. Some of these include states complemented by capitols, the National Football League or collegiate teams complemented by their mascot, or cartoon characters and their rivals. For example, the standard *dive* play can be called *Denver*, and the complementing *dive-option* play can be called *Colorado*. The *toss sweep* can be called *Arkansas*, and the sweep pass can be called *Razorback*. These are just a couple of examples of how offensive systems can adapt their verbal calls to the hurry-up philosophy.

Signaling of Plays

After establishing the verbal communication for all your plays, the next step is to identify physical motions that you can associate with each play. The following four attributes represent a quality physical signaling system:

- The system must be simple.
- The system must be quick.
- The movements must relate to the play.
- The motions must be easily seen and understood.

Simplicity is the most important aspect of your physical signaling motions. If a signal is too complicated with any possibility of misreading it, then it should be changed. A good signal system can also be relayed quickly and accurately. This will allow the signaling coach to relay the plays to your quarterback at a fast pace. Your physical signals cannot slow down the pace of the game. You shouldn't worry about other coaches stealing your signals due to their simplicity. This concern will be addressed later in this chapter. Be sure each physical signal complements its verbal one, because this insures easier recall by your players.

Remember, when teaching the signal communication system with the verbal command of the quarterback, make sure you associate a story, phrase, or anecdote for better memorization by your athletes. This technique should trigger a thought pattern that will reinforce the play that you are relaying. Finally, the offensive players should easily see the motions in your signaling. Each motion should be distinct, separate, and not even remotely similar to any other motion. Again, if any possibility for miscommunication exists, then the motion needs to be changed.

You should make sure that all your offensive coaches have the ability to signal every play. They can practice this during individual, inside, or outside offensive periods. This will also help you in case one of your signalers becomes ill during the course of the season.

Figure 4-4: Moses
Holding his staff

Figure 4-5: Egypt
Egyptian Pose

Figure 4-6: Daniel
On his knees praying

Figure 4-7: Lion
Lion's pose

Figure 4-8a: David
Slinging his slingshot

Figure 4-8b: David
Slinging his slingshot

Figure 4-9: Giant
Big and strong

Figure 4-10: John
John stuck in prison

Figure 4-11: Baptist
Praying

Figure 4-12: Behead
Cutting of Head

Figure 4-13: Noah
Buidling the ark

Figure 4-14: Ark
Floating in water

Figure 4-15a: Joshua
Walked around Jericho

Figure 4-15b: Joshua
Walked around Jericho

Figure 4-16: Roman
Roman soldier

Figure 4-17: Peter
Walking

Figure 4-18: Water
Wave

Coaches' Responsibilities

To be able to call plays effectively at such fast pace in the hurry-up, you have to have an organized approach to calling plays within your offensive staff. You should have your coaches responsible for four specific duties during a game. They are the *play caller*, the *passing-game coordinator*, the *running-game coordinator*, and the *play-calling board* coach.

Play Caller

- He is the person who will actually call the plays during the game
- He should be the coach who knows the offensive system the best.
- He has to have the game plan memorized well enough to call plays at a fast pace, under pressure, according to down-and-distance, and to know what the defense is giving the offensive on every down.
- If you have a well-organized and simple offensive system, this job will be a lot easier than it sounds.

Coaching Point:

- When calling the play, the coach should talk through the signaler to the board coach. This will ensure that the defense cannot pick up what the play will be. The play caller must know his offensive system well enough to know what to call based on the potential of limited information from the passing- and running-game coordinator.

Passing-Game Coordinator

- He is the person responsible for signaling in the plays.
- He needs to know the passing game inside and out, including all of your coverage rules and quarterback reads.
- He needs to be able to recognize defensive coverages and be able to tell the play caller what pass coverages the defense is showing you. This will be his biggest job.
- He is responsible for relaying the defensive-coverage tendencies to the play caller. For example, on third and long, he should look for cover 3.
- He will also relay the down-and-distance after each play is finished.

Coaching Points:

- The passing-game coordinator, or the signaler, will need to wear a different color shirt or hat to be seen by the quarterback quickly.

- The signaler will only relay the specific defensive coverages to the play caller while you have the ball. He will not verbalize the actual plays that are open to the play caller. This will help the offense move at a faster pace and will not overload the play caller with too much information from the passing- and running-game coordinators.
- During timeouts and when the defense is on the field are the proper times when the signaler will give the play caller the actual plays that should be open. The play caller can then circle these particular plays on the game-plan sheet and be ready for the next series.
- The signaler will wait until the play-calling board coach has flipped the color and numbers before giving the signal. This will again limit the defense's ability to figure out the next play.

Running-Game Coordinator

- He is the person who needs to know the running game inside and out, including your blocking scheme and its rules versus different defensive fronts.
- He will need to be able to recognize the defensive front you're seeing and where the stunts and blitzes are coming from to be able to tell the play caller what running coverages the defense is showing you. This will be his biggest job.
- He will also be in charge of your pass-protection schemes since he will have the job of recognizing blitzes and stunts.

Coaching Points:

- The running-game coordinator will only relay the specific defensive front's tendencies to the play caller while you have the ball. He will not verbalize the actual running plays that will work against the defense. This will help the offense move at a faster pace and will not overload the play caller with too much information from the passing- and running-game coordinators.
- During timeouts and when the defense is on the field are the proper times for the signaler to give the play caller the actual plays that should be open. The play caller can then circle these particular plays on the game-plan sheet and be ready for the next series.

Play-Calling Board Coach

- He is the person who will work the color and the first number on your play-calling board. This is an extremely important job since the color gives the information to the player on whether to look at the board or to the signaler.
- He will be in charge of the backup quarterback who helps run the last two numbers on the board. This job can prepare a younger quarterback to handle the hurry-up communication system in years to come.

- The board coach needs to have the ability to work quickly under pressure. This can be the most stressful position of your four offensive coaches involved in this communication system.

Coaching Point:

- When the signaler is *hot* and is actually giving the play, put up the numbers to some of your most often used pass plays. This will cut down on the defense's ability to pick up your offensive tendencies.

Staff Alignment

Having complete staff alignment is extremely important among your coaches. It ensures consistency for your players for them to recognize where to look for the next play without confusion. The play-calling board coach is the one responsible for the entire staff alignment on the sideline. He should set the board up 10-yards behind the placement of the ball. The signaler will align next to the board on its color side so the players can look in the general direction of the play, without giving the defense any indication of whether they are looking at the board or the signaler. The play caller will be next to the signaler. As mentioned before, the play caller should always talk through the signaler to the board. Finally, the running-game coordinator will align next to the play caller on the very outside; this will put him in a good position to not only communicate with the play caller, but also gives him a good view and perspective of the defensive front (Figures 4-19 and 4-20).

Figure 4-19

RUNNING GAME COORDINATOR
GAME TENDENCY CHART

DOWN AND DISTANCE	DEFENSIVE FRONT	STUNTS/BLITZS

PASSING GAME COORDINATOR
GAME TENDENCY CHART

DOWN AND DISTANCE	PRE-SNAP COVERAGE	ACTUAL COVERAGE WITH BLITZS

Figure 4-20

Players' Responsibilities

Once you've learned and understand your coaches' responsibilities, you can focus on your players' roles within the hurry-up communication system. Not only does your coaches' communication system need to be organized and precise, your players also have to know their assignments in the communication system and carry out their roles to be a successful team. Every team puts a lot of pressure on their quarterbacks. If your quarterback plays well on game day, your entire team will usually play well. Within this communication system, the quarterback is just as important as any coach. He is the man who makes the system work.

Quarterback

- He is the person who needs to know all your signals.
- He has to verbally relay the proper formation to his teammates.
- He must interpret the key color on the play-calling board, and if it is a running play, he reinforces it two or three times. But if the key color is a pass play, then he will give a false call, which tells the receivers to look at the board.
- If any motion is signaled in, the quarterback must verbally relay it to the appropriate receiver.
- After recognizing the possibility that a play will not be successful, the quarterback has to have the ability to audible the correct play.
- His last step is to call the cadence in a rhythmic manner.

Coaching Point:

- Before every game, the signaler and the quarterbacks will review all signals to reinforce their memory.

Backs and Receivers

- These are the people who must be able to read the numbers on the play-calling board.
- They must look towards the sideline the same amount of time throughout a game regardless of reading a pass play on the board or hearing the quarterback call a running play.
- They must listen for an audible indicating a change in the play.
- They must be able to recognize the color key and all the signals in case it ever gets so loud during a game that it is tough to hear the quarterback.
- They must listen for and anticipate the cadence.

Linemen

- They are the people who must listen to the quarterback verbalize a running play or the false call to identify a pass.
- When it is a pass, they must listen for the fullback to make a pass-protection call according to the defensive alignment.
- They must listen for any audible indicating a change in the play.
- The offensive tackles must be able to recognize the color key and all the signals in case it ever gets so loud during a game that it is tough to hear the quarterback.
- They must listen for and anticipate the cadence.

Player Alignment

Your quarterback should align 10-yards directly behind where the ball is spotted, and should then face the coaches on the sideline awaiting the formation and play call. After a play is completed, the backs and receivers should hustle back to the line of scrimmage, aiming to the center of the field, while awaiting the quarterback's call of the formation. This puts them in a better position to get into formation at a quicker pace. While running to the appropriate side of the formation, they must look at the play-calling board and listen for the play. It is important that they hustle to be set up, know their assignment, and have time to recognize defensive alignment before the ball is snapped. The center needs to understand that he is the key for the entire line to get set up properly at a fast pace. Linemen will set up on the center's feet while he is waiting for the official to place the ball.

CHAPTER 5

How to Practice the Hurry-Up, No-Huddle

It is imperative that you incorporate the hurry-up philosophy into all phases of your practice schedule. Three specific areas of practice in which you should do this are: *your team*, *inside periods*, and *outside periods*. By applying the hurry-up to all facets of your practices, you will program your coaches and players to execute the offense at a much quicker pace that will carry over to your game days.

The Team-Versus-Air Drill

During this practice period, you will have all 11 offensive players out on the field, with your coaches on the sideline signaling plays. Your offensive unit will go up and down the field simulating an actual series of plays, but at a much faster pace than in a real game. This will acclimate your players and coaches to thinking and executing at a faster pace than normal. This will also allow your coaches to recognize and correct any minor communication mistakes that could occur in a game. You want your game days to seem slow when compared to the *team-versus-air drill* (see Figure 5-1).

Players' Responsibilities

The players will have the same responsibilities that they have on game days.

Quarterback

The quarterback will align 10-yards behind where the ball is spotted, look to the sideline, receive the play, and then reinforce it verbally to his teammates. Next, he will look to make sure the offensive team is properly aligned and set, call out the cadence, and execute the play. After each play, he will hustle to the area directly behind the ball and repeat this process.

Backs and Receivers

The backs and receivers need to listen for the formation, and while moving into position, listen for the play and execute the assignment when the ball is snapped. After the play is over, they will hustle towards the line of scrimmage where the ball is spotted and repeat the process.

Linemen

The linemen will get their proper splits on the center, listen for the play, and execute it. After the play is over, the center must find where the umpire will spot the ball and get set up quickly so the rest of the linemen can also get aligned properly. A center that does not do his job can slow a team down greatly.

Coaches' Responsibilities

This is the best drill for your coaching staff because it is the closest thing that resembles actual game-day situations.

Staff Alignment

Your staff will be aligned exactly like they would be in a game. First, the play-calling board coach will align the board 10-yards behind where the ball is spotted, angling towards the ball. Next to the board will be the signaler, followed by the play caller, and lastly the running-game coordinator.

Signaling in Formations and Plays

The passing-game coordinator will get the formation from the play caller. He will be facing the quarterback and signaling the formation into him. While the quarterback is reinforcing the formation to his teammates, he identifies the key color that tells him whether to look at the board or the signaler for the play. After receiving the play, he verbally reinforces it to his teammates. The quarterback will take one last look to the sidelines to see if any motion is necessary for the play.

Getting the Proper Personnel into the Game

The running-game coordinator is responsible for all personnel groups ready to enter a game. He does this by having them stand behind him, listening for their particular formation or play. The way they will recognize this is to listen for the play caller to call out the formation or personnel group out loud to the signaler.

Ball Spotter Responsibilities

This is a very important job that you should assign an assistant coach to do. He will act as if he is an actual referee. He will have two footballs. He will spot one as soon as he whistles the play dead. After placing the ball down, he will become the umpire and your players will give the ball to him just like they would in a regular game. He will spot the ball in the proper place according to where the ball is blown dead, moving it from hash to hash. He will work as if it is a regular game as far as penalties and incomplete passes are concerned.

When to Practice the Team-Versus-Air Drill

This is the first drill to incorporate when implementing the hurry-up, no-huddle. You should do this drill everyday in preseason practices, including the beginning and the end before conditioning. The first time you run this drill you should only use one formation and two or three plays to keep it simple enough for coaches and players to execute and have a positive experience. Slowly add formations and plays at a pace that your team can handle. After one week, you should be able to communicate your entire offensive system. This may seem like a major challenge, but you can do it with hard work and concentration. During the season, you may only want to practice the team-versus-air drill on the last practice before each game. If you're not meeting your goals for speeding up the game, then you should practice it everyday if necessary.

The Outside-Versus-Secondary Drill

This is the same drill that many teams already have in their practice schedule, but you will be adding the hurry-up pace to it. You will use your quarterback, center, and five receivers versus seven scout-team defenders. You will run your main pass plays versus each particular coverage that you might see in a game. By adding the hurry-up pace,

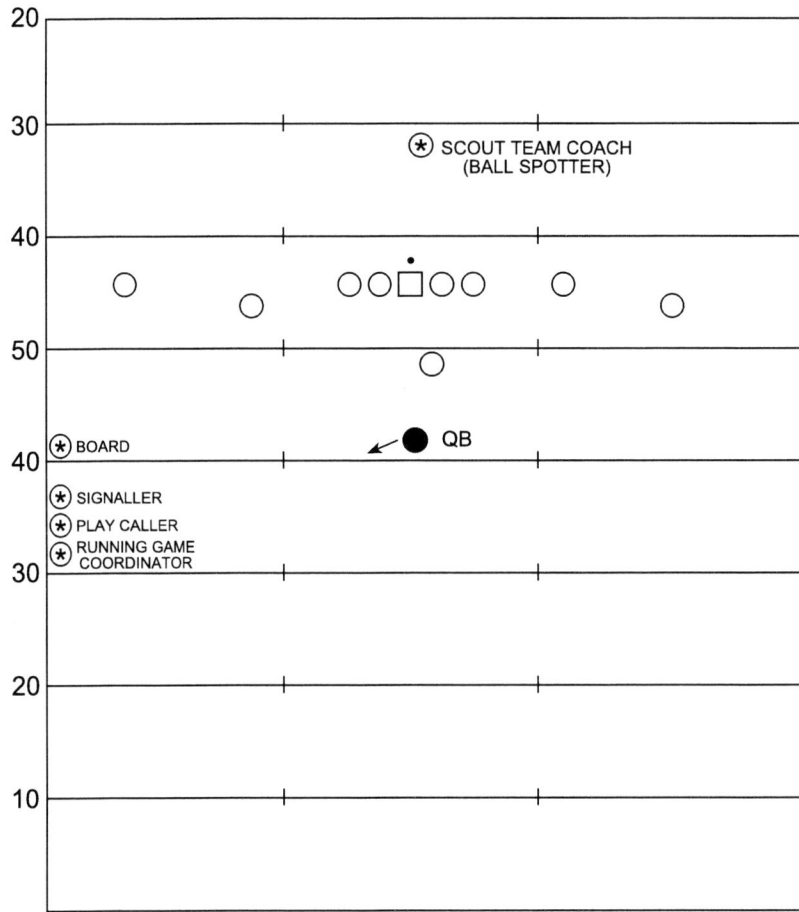

Figure 5-1: Team vs. Air

you should be able to get twice as many repetitions as before when running this drill. If you are not achieving this, then you need to pick up the pace (See Figure 5-2).

Players' Responsibilities

After the quarterback gives the formation and the play, your players will be asked to execute the play. When the play is over, the players will hustle back to the line of scrimmage toward the ball, listening for the quarterback to give the next formation so backs and receivers can go to that side of the field. This will help program your backs and receivers into the timing of the hurry-up communication system. A key aspect will be for the receivers to not retrieve any incomplete passes. This will drastically slow down the pace of the drill. Instead, they will hustle back to the line of scrimmage just like they would do in a game. Use your managers to retrieve the incomplete passes during this drill.

Coaches' Responsibilities

The passing-game coordinator will be in charge of running this drill. This drill is not only great for players, but it is also great practice for your coaches, especially the passing-game coordinator who will be signaling to the quarterback on game days.

The coach's alignment will be 10-yards behind the ball, off to the quarterback's side at the same angle that he would be during a game. His first job is to signal or verbally tell the quarterback the formation and the play. To keep the pace quick, he must call the formation and play as soon as the previous play is completed, and before the receivers get back to the line of scrimmage. If you are taking more than 25 seconds after a complete or incomplete pass, then you are running this drill too slowly.

Another responsibility for the coach is to control the competitiveness of this drill. If you want a more competitive drill, the passing-game coordinator can align behind the defensive scout team and relay the formation verbally and the play silently to the offensive players. This will keep the defensive scout team honest and not allow them to know which play is being run.

Another coaching responsibility is for someone to be the scout-team coach. The scout-team coach's alignment will be six to seven yards in front of the ball where the umpire position is during a regular game. He will be in charge of the scout-defensive secondary and will relay to them the proper coverage. He will also act as the official, but he will be working with two footballs. As soon as one play is over, he will throw the center the ball, and the player that caught the completed pass will hand the remaining ball to him like they would in a regular game. This will help program your players to hand the ball to the official after the play is run.

Coaching Point:

- When making coaching points or demonstrating a technique in this drill, you should jump right in to make your point and get right out again so you don't slow down the pace of the drill. Remember, the major teaching of passing routes, reads, and timing should occur at the slower pace of an individual period.

Scout-Team Responsibilities

The scout team should line up in the proper coverage given by the scout-team coach. As soon as one play is over, they need to get back into position quickly. These players

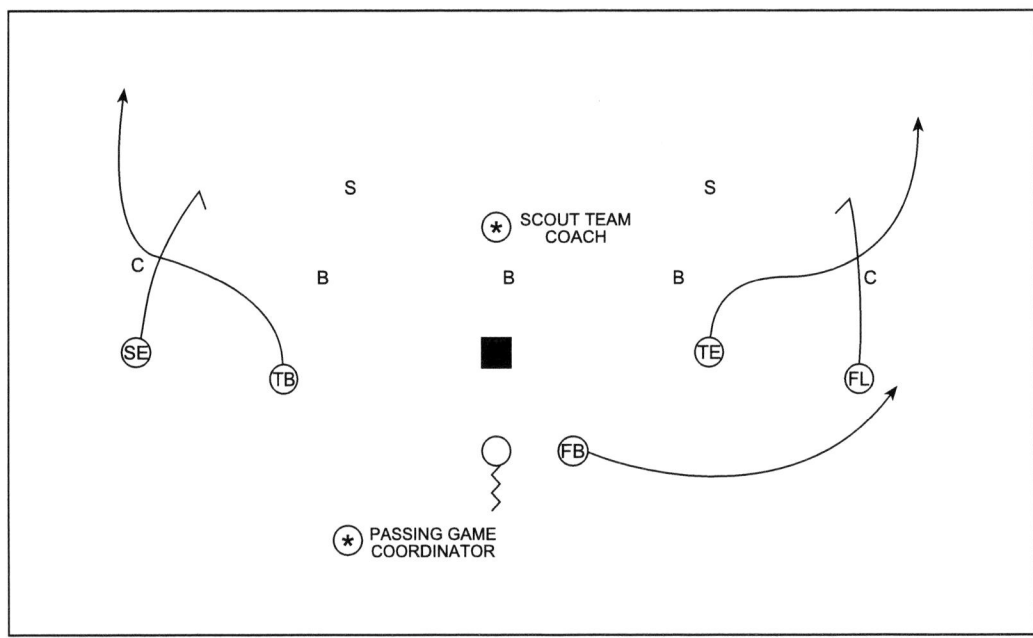

Figure 5-2a: Outside vs. Secondary-Step 1

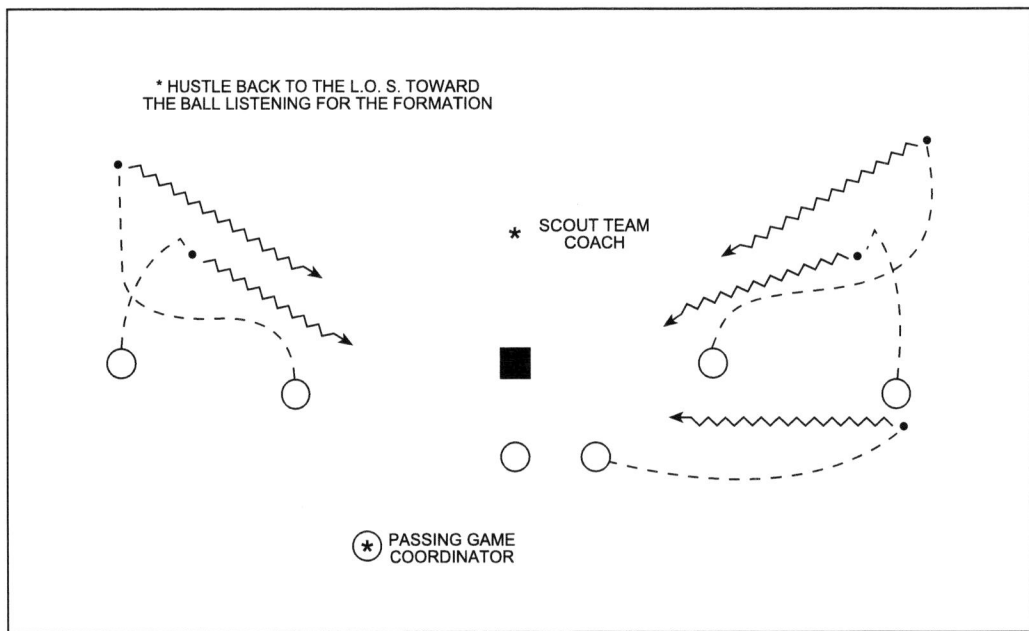

Figure 5-2b: Outside vs. Secondary-Step 2

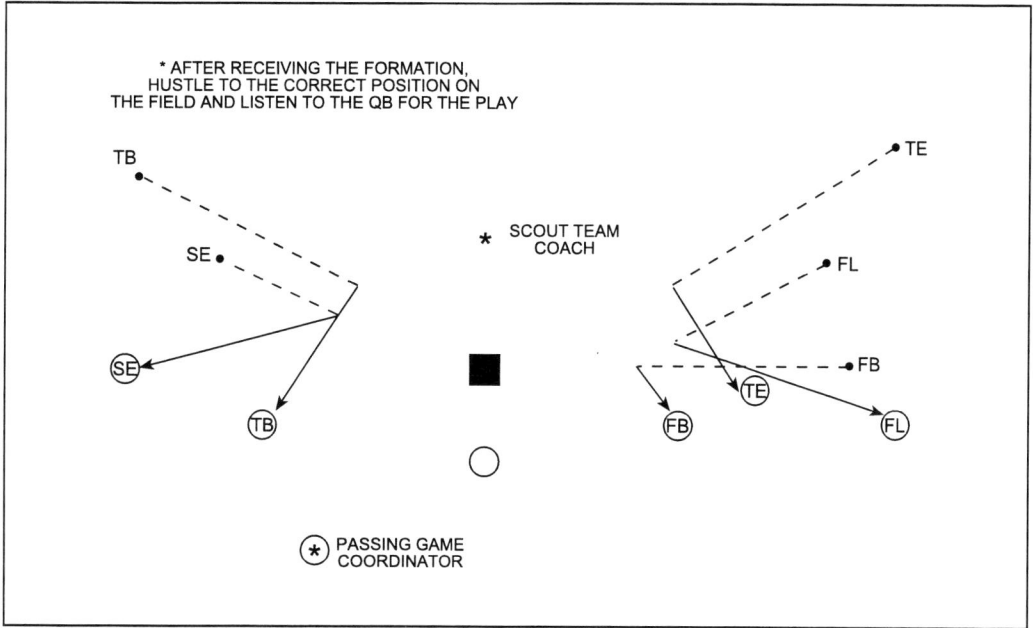

Figure 5-2c: Outside vs. Secondary-Step 3

cannot slow down the pace of the drill. They need to be instructed to the level of competitiveness that the passing-game coordinator wants. Whether it is full speed tackling, pro-style knock-up, or just breaking on the ball with no contact.

Coaching Point:

- You should make sure the scout team wears a different color practice jersey, pullover, or beanie to help the quarterback see the difference in the players when making his reads.

The Inside-Versus-Front-Seven Drill

This is another drill that many teams already have in their practice schedule, but again, you will be adding the hurry-up pace to the drill. You will use your quarterback, two backs, and five offensive linemen versus seven scout-team defenders. You will run your main running plays versus each particular defensive front that you might see in a game. By adding the hurry-up pace, you should be able to get twice as many repetitions as before when running this drill. If you are not achieving this, then you need to pick up the pace (See Figure 5-3).

Players' Responsibilities

After the quarterback relays the formation and the play, your players will be asked to execute the play. When the play is over, the players will hustle back to the line of scrimmage, listening for the quarterback to give the next formation, with the center catching the ball from the scout-team coach and spotting the ball so the rest of the linemen can get into position according to his alignment. This will help program your backs and receivers into the timing of the hurry-up communication system. A key aspect for the linemen will be to get set as soon as possible to hear the play and make their line calls before the quarterback begins his cadence.

Coaches' Responsibilities

The running-game coordinator will be in charge of running this drill. This drill is not only great for players, but it is also great practice for your coaches, especially the running-game coordinator who will be the one recognizing defensive fronts and giving plays to the play caller on game days.

His alignment will be 10-yards behind the ball, off to the quarterback's side at the same angle that he would be during a game. His first job is to signal or verbally tell the quarterback the formation and the play. To keep the pace quick, he must call the formation and play as soon as the previous play is completed, and before the linemen get back to the line of scrimmage. If you are taking more than 25 seconds after a play is finished, then you are running this drill too slow.

Another responsibility for the coach is to control the competitiveness of this drill. If you want a more competitive drill, the running-game coordinator can align behind the defensive scout team and relay the formation verbally and the play silently to the offensive players. This will keep the defensive scout team honest and will not allow them to know which play is being run.

Coaching Point:

- When making coaching points or demonstrating a technique in this drill, you should jump right in to make your point and get right out again so you don't slow down the pace of the drill. Remember, the major teaching of passing routes, reads, and timing should occur at the slower pace of an individual period.

Scout-Team Responsibilities

The scout team should line up in the proper fronts given by the scout-team coach. As soon as one play is over, they need to get back into position as soon as possible. These players cannot slow down the pace of the drill. They need to be instructed to the level of competitiveness that the running game coordinator wants whether it is full speed tackling, pro-style knock-up, or just holding dummies.

Coaching Point:

- Make sure the scout team wears a different color practice jersey, pullover, or beanie to help the running backs see the difference in the players when making their cuts.
- Many coaches ask how they are supposed to run these drills at the hurry-up pace, and at the same time expect their players to execute their techniques and assignments effectively enough to have a successful offense. The answer is to make sure and teach proper techniques and assignments during individual periods everyday in practice, during team meetings before or after practice, during the off-season for about twenty minutes a day, and three days a week during your summer workouts. This will give your players more than enough repetitions to execute the hurry-up pace properly and consistently.

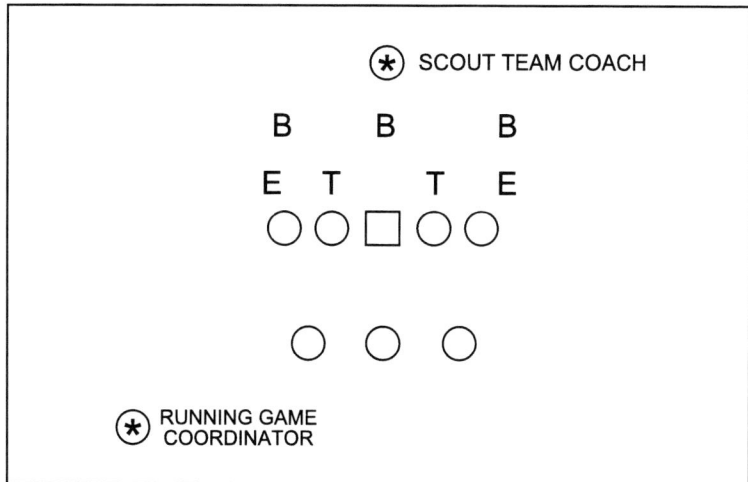

Figure 5-3: Inside Drill

Sample Practice Schedules

Day: Monday **Dress:** Shorts/Shoulder Pads/Helmets **Notes:** Four full-length gassers

TIME	COMMENTS	QB	FB	TB	TE	SE	FL	O-LINE
2:45	Stretch with individual coaches	Warm Up Arm						
2:50		w/FB 1 and 2 routes	Ball Drills	Ball Drills	Ball Drills	Ball Drills	Ball Drills	
2:55		w/TB 1 and 2 routes	Ball Drills	w/QB 1 and 2 routes	1 and 2 routes/no QB	Releases	Stock Block	Step Drill
3:00	Individual Offense	w/TE 1 and 2 routes	1-on-1 Pass Protection	Stock Block	w/QB 1 and 2 routes	0 and 1 routes/no QB	Releases	1-on-1 Pass Protection
3:05		w/SE 0 and 1 routes	Team Pass Protection	Releases	Stock Block	w/QB 0 and 1 routes	0 and 1 routes/no QB	Team Pass Protection
3:10		w/FL 0 and 1 routes	Team Pass Protection	1 and 2 routes/no QB	Releases	Stock Block	w/QB 0 and 1 routes	Team Pass Protection
3:15	Inside Drill vs Dummies and Outside Drill vs Scout	No. 1's Inside/No. 2's Outside	**	**	**	**	**	No. 1's Inside/No. 2's Scout
3:20	Four Base Runs vs Even Front	No. 1's Inside/No. 2's Outside	**	**	**	**	**	No. 1's Inside/No. 2's Scout
3:25	Four Base Passes vs Cover 3	No. 1's Inside/No. 2's Outside	**	**	**	**	**	No. 1's Inside/No. 2's Scout
3:30	Inside Drill vs Dummies Outside Drill vs Scout	No. 2's Inside/No. 1's Outside		**	**	**	**	No. 1's Inside/No. 2's Scout
3:35		No. 2's Inside/No. 1's Outside	**	**	**	**	**	No. 2's Inside/No. 1's Scout
3:40	No. 1's and No. 2's Switch	No. 2's Inside/No. 1's Outside	**	**	**	**	**	**
3:45	Break	TEAM	TEAM	TEAM	TEAM	TEAM	TEAM	TEAM
3:50	Team-Screen Period	1's*	**	**	**	**	**	**
3:55	Outside screens to both sides	1's	**	**	**	**	**	**
4:00		2's	**	**	**	**	**	**
4:05	Team Offense	1's	**	**	**	**	**	**
4:10	Introduce Opponent's Base Defense and Game Plan	1's	**	**	**	**	**	**
4:15		2's	**	**	**	**	**	**
4:20	Break	TEAM	TEAM	TEAM	TEAM	TEAM	TEAM	TEAM
4:25	Special Plays	1's	**	**	**	**	**	**
4:30	Two different plays each day	1's	**	**	**	**	**	**
4:35	Hurry-Up, No-Huddle	1's	**	**	**	**	**	**
4:40	Team vs Air	2's	**	**	**	**	**	**
4:45	Conditioning	TEAM	TEAM	TEAM	TEAM	TEAM	TEAM	TEAM

Day: Tuesday **Dress:** Full Pads **Notes:** Four full-length gassers

TIME	COMMENTS	QB	FB	TB	TE	SE	FL	O-LINE
2:45	Stretch	Warm Up Arm						
2:50	with individual coaches	w/FB 3 and 4 routes	Ball Drills	Ball Drills	Ball Drills	Ball Drills	Ball Drills	
2:55		w/TB 5 and 6 routes	Ball Drills	w/QB 5 and 6 routes	Ball Drills	Releases	Stalk Block	Step Drill
3:00	Individual Offense	w/TE 5 and 6 routes	1-on-1 Pass Protection	Stalk Block	5 and 6 routes/no QB	3 and 4 routes/no QB	Releases	1-on-1 Pass Protection
3:05		w/SE 3 and 4 routes	Team Pass Protection	Releases	w/QB 5 and 6 routes	w/QB 3 and 4 routes	3 and 4 routes/no QB	Team Pass Protection
3:10		w/FL 3 and 4 routes	Team Pass Protection	5 and 6 routes/no QB	Stalk Block	Stalk Block	w/QB 3 and 4 routes	Team Pass Protection
3:15	Inside Drill vs Scout and	No. 1's Inside/No. 1's Outside	**	**	**	**	**	No. 1's Inside/No. 2's Scout
3:20	Outside Drill vs Scout Four Base Runs vs Odd Front	No. 1's Inside/No. 2's Outside	**	**	**	**	**	No. 1's Inside/No. 2's Scout
3:25	Pro Tempo Four Base Passes vs Cover 2 and 4	No. 1's Inside/No. 2's Outside	**	**	**	**	**	No. 1's Inside/No. 1's Scout
3:30	Inside Drill vs Scout	No. 2's Inside/No. 1's Outside	**	**	**	**	**	No. 1's Inside/No. 2's Scout
3:35	Outside Drill vs Scout	No. 2's Inside/No. 1's Outside	**	**	**	**	**	No. 2's Inside/No. 1's Scout
3:40	No. 1's and No. 2's Switch	No. 2's Inside/No. 1's Outside	**	**	**	**	**	**
3:45	Break	TEAM	TEAM	TEAM	TEAM	TEAM	TEAM	TEAM
3:50	Team-Screen Period	1's	**	**	**	**	**	**
3:55	Inside screens to both sides	1's	**	**	**	**	**	**
4:00		2's	**	**	**	**	**	**
4:05	Team Offense	1's	**	**	**	**	**	**
4:10	Opponent's Base Defense	1's	**	**	**	**	**	**
4:15	with Blitzes	2's	**	**	**	**	**	**
4:20	Break	TEAM	TEAM	TEAM	TEAM	TEAM	TEAM	TEAM
4:25	Special Plays	1's	**	**	**	**	**	**
4:30	Two different plays each day	1's	**	**	**	**	**	**
4:35	Hurry-Up, No-Huddle	1's	**	**	**	**	**	**
4:40	Team vs Air	2's	**	**	**	**	**	**
4:45	Conditioning	TEAM	TEAM					

Day: Wednesday Dress: Full Pads Notes: Four full-length gassers

TIME	COMMENTS	QB	FB	TB	TE	SE	FL	O-LINE
2:45	Stretch with individual coaches	Warm Up Arm	Stretch	Stretch	Stretch	Stretch	Stretch	Stretch
2:50	Individual Offense	w/FB 3 and 4 routes	Ball Drills	Ball Drills	Ball Drills	Ball Drills	Ball Drills	Stance Drill
2:55		w/TB 5 and 6 routes	Ball Drills	w/QB 5 and 6 routes	5 and 6 routes/no QB	Releases	Stalk Block	Step Drill
3:00		w/TE 5 and 6 routes	1-on-1 Pass Protection	Stalk Block	w/QB 5 and 6 routes	3 and 4 routes/no QB	Releases	1-on-1 Pass Protection
3:05		w/SE 3 and 4 routes	Team Pass Protection	Releases	Stalk Block	w/QB 3 and 4 routes/no QB	3 and 4 routes/no QB	Team Pass Protection
3:10		w/FL 3 and 4 routes	Team Pass Protection	5 and 6 routes/no QB	Releases	Stalk Block	w/QB 3 and 4 routes	Team Pass Protection
3:15	Inside Drill vs Scout and Outside Drill vs Scout	No. 1's Inside	No. 1's Inside	No. 1's Inside	No. 1's Inside	No. 1's Inside	No. 1's Inside	No. 1's Inside
3:20	Four Base Runs vs Both Fronts w/Blitzes Pro Tempo	No. 2's Outside	No. 2's Outside	No. 2's Outside	No. 2's Outside	No. 2's Outside	No. 2's Outside	No. 2's Outside
3:25	Four Base Passes vs Man Coverages							
3:30	Inside Drill vs Scout	No. 2's Inside	No. 2's Inside	No. 2's Inside	No. 2's Inside	No. 2's Inside	No. 2's Inside	No. 2's Inside
3:35	Outside Drill vs Scout	No. 1's Outside	No. 1's Outside	No. 1's Outside	No. 1's Outside	No. 1's Outside	No. 1's Outside	No. 1's Outside
3:40	No. 1's and No. 2's Switch							
3:45	Break	TEAM	TEAM	TEAM	TEAM	TEAM	TEAM	TEAM
3:50	Team Run Period vs Opponent's Base Defense	1's	1's	1's	1's	1's	1's	1's
3:55		2's	2's	2's	2's	2's	2's	2's
4:00								
4:05	Team Offense Opponent's Base Defense with Blitzes	1's	1's	1's	1's	1's	1's	1's
4:10								
4:15								
4:20	Break	TEAM	TEAM	TEAM	TEAM	TEAM	TEAM	TEAM
4:25	Special Plays Two different plays each day	1's	1's	1's	1's	1's	1's	1's
4:30								
4:35	Hurry-Up, No-Huddle Team vs Air	1's	1's	1's	1's	1's	1's	1's
4:40		2's	2's	2's	2's	2's	2's	2's
4:45	Conditioning	TEAM	TEAM	TEAM	TEAM	TEAM	TEAM	TEAM

Day: Thursday **Dress:** Shoulders/Helmets

TIME	COMMENTS	QB	FB	TB	TE	SE	FL	O-LINE
2:45	Stretch as a team	Warm Up Arm	Team Stretch	Team Stretch	Team Stretch	Team Stretch	Team Stretch	Team Stretch
2:50								
2:55	Inside Drill vs Opponent's Base Defense	No. 1's Inside	No. 1's Inside	No. 1's Inside	No. 1's Inside	No. 1's Inside	No. 1's Inside	No. 1's Inside
3:00	Outside Drill vs. Opponent's Base Coverage	No. 2's Outside	No. 2's Outside	No. 2's Outside	No. 2's Outside	No. 2's Outside	No. 2's Outside	No. 2's Outside
3:05								
3:10	Inside Drill vs Opponent's Base Defense	No. 2's Inside	No. 2's Inside	No. 2's Inside	No. 2's Inside	No. 2's Inside	No. 2's Inside	No. 2's Inside
3:15	Outside Drill vs. Opponent's Base Coverage	No. 1's Outside	No. 1's Outside	No. 1's Outside	No. 1's Outside	No. 1's Outside	No. 1's Outside	No. 1's Outside
3:20								
3:25	Red Zone Offense	1's	1's	1's	1's	1's	1's	1's
3:30								
3:35	Hurry-Up, No-Huddle Team vs Air	1's	1's	1's	1's	1's	1's	1's
3:40								
3:45								
3:50	End	2's	2's	2's	2's	2's	2's	2's
3:55								
4:00								
4:05								
4:10								
4:15								
4:20								
4:25								
4:30								
4:35								
4:40								
4:45								

CHAPTER 6

The Hurry-Up, No-Huddle Running Game

This chapter illustrates four main running plays in the hurry-up offense, including player responsibilities and coaching points for each play.

The Counter Trey

When implementing the *counter trey*, your goal is to build a wall inside, kick-out the edge, and wrap through for the frontside linebacker in the box. You should direct this play to the 1 technique or shade the noseguard to gain a free release by the frontside tackle to the backside linebacker. You can run this versus six in the box or less (Figures 6-1 through 6-4). The frontside keys in the counter trey are as follows:

- If the inside gap is covered by a down lineman, he is basically the guard's and tackle's responsibility.
- If the inside gap is uncovered, the tackle will track to the backside linebacker.

Player Responsibilities:

- FST—He should double with the guard versus a 2 or 3 technique. If he is uncovered, he should track to the second linebacker in the box.

- FSG—He should double with the tackle versus a 2 or 3 technique. He should also be watching for the backside linebacker to run through.
- C—He should block back on first down lineman backside.
- BSG—He should kick-out first thing and head-up to the outside frontside tackle.
- BST—He should wrap through for the playside linebacker in the box.
- QB—He should carry out a boot fake to hold the backside defensive end.
- Variation—He can switch the responsibilities with the backside tackle and running back to get to the counter GB.

Coaching Points:

- You must establish movement on the double-team versus a 2 or 3 technique.
- The center must maintain a solid back block.
- The aiming point is from the frontside B gap to the frontside A gap.

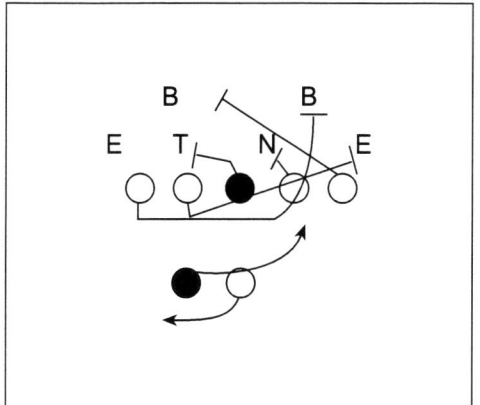

Figure 6-1: Counter Trey

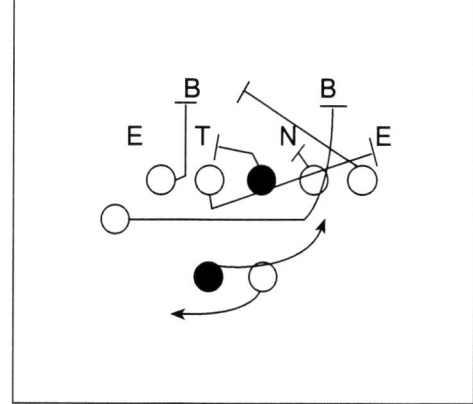

Figure 6-2: Counter GB (Guard & Back)

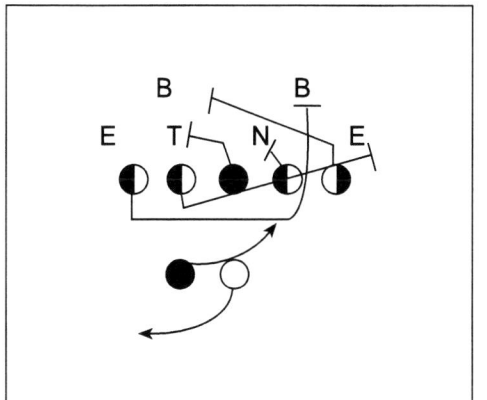

Figure 6-3a: Counter Trey vs. 4-2

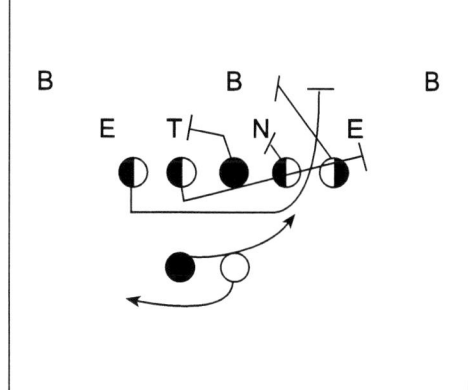

Figure 6-3b: Counter Trey vs. 4-1

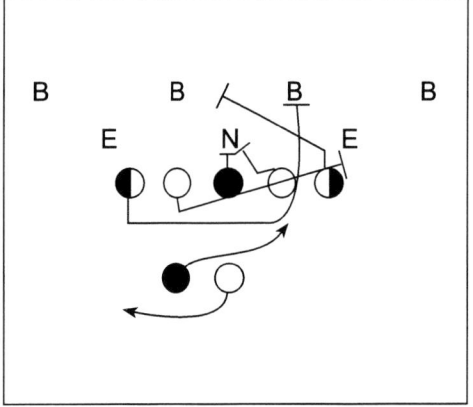

Figure 6-3c: Counter Trey vs. 3-2

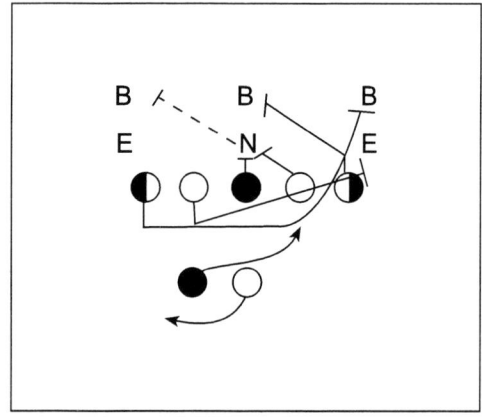

Figure 6-3d: Counter Trey vs. 3-3

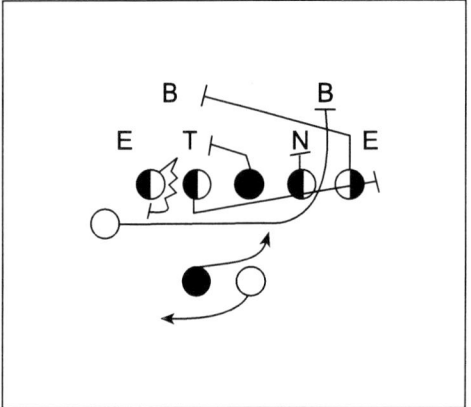

Figure 6-4a: Counter GB vs. 4-2

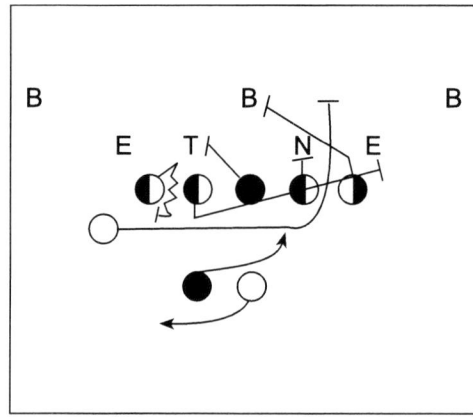

Figure 6-4b: Counter GB vs. 4-1

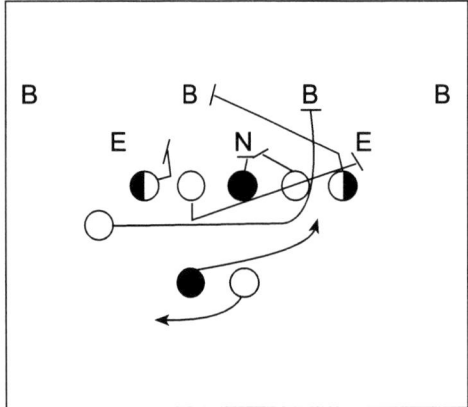

Figure 6-4c: Counter GB vs. 3-2

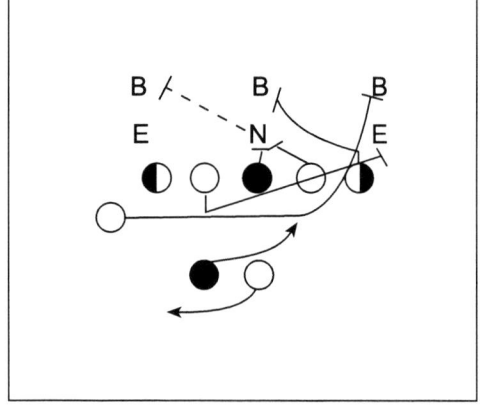

Figure 6-4d: Counter GB vs. 3-3

The Trap

When implementing the *trap*, your goal is to separate the defense by taking advantage of the interior defensive lineman alignments. You should gain an element of surprise by snapping the ball directly to the running back. You can direct this play to the widest interior lineman (i.e., the 3 technique). If you are presented with two techniques, the quarterback should pick a side to utilize the best trapping guard. You can run this versus 6 in the box or less (Figures 6-5 and 6-6).

Player Responsibilities:

- FST—He should escape the defensive end and block the linebacker head-up to the outside.
- FSG—He should slip to the interior lineman and block the linebacker head-up to the backside.
- C—He should snap the ball directly to the running back and block back for the trapping guard.
- BSG—He should pull flat off the center's rear and trap the first down lineman past the center.
- BST—He should escape the defensive end and block the linebacker head-up to the outside.
- RB—He should catch the direct snap on the run and stay midline.
- QB—He should act as if the snap went over his head.

Coaching Points:

- The trapping guard must pull flat into the line of scrimmage to ensure a good inside-out kick-out.
- The center must snap the ball waist high to hide it from the defense.
- The tackles must take slightly wider than normal splits to remove the defensive end from the play.

The Sweep

When implementing the *sweep*, your goal is to set the edge and get the ball to the perimeter quickly with two lead blockers. You should run this to a 1, 2, or 3 technique. You can run this versus six in the box or less (Figures 6-7 and 6-8).

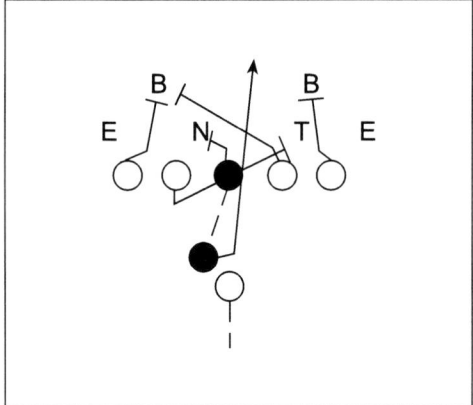

Figure 6-5: Trap

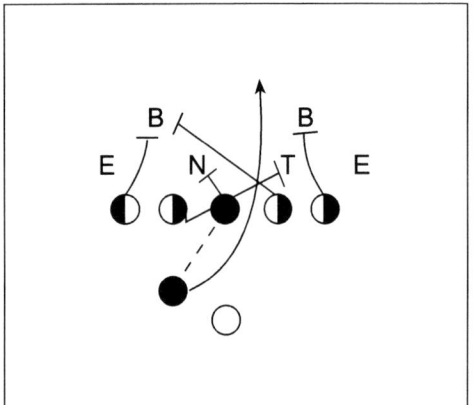

Figure 6-6a: Trap vs. 4-2

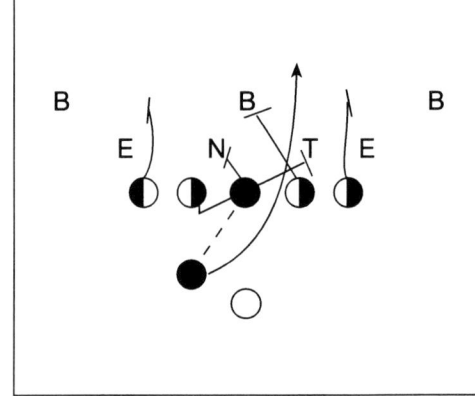

Figure 6-6b: Trap vs. 4-1

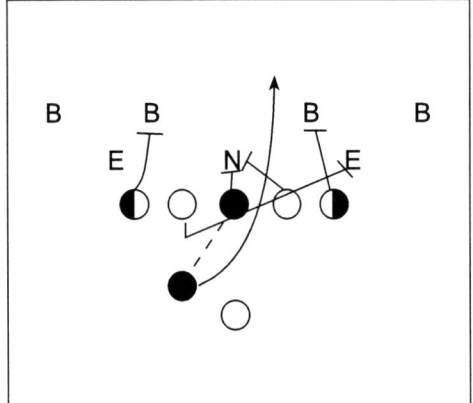

Figure 6-6c: Trap vs. 3-2

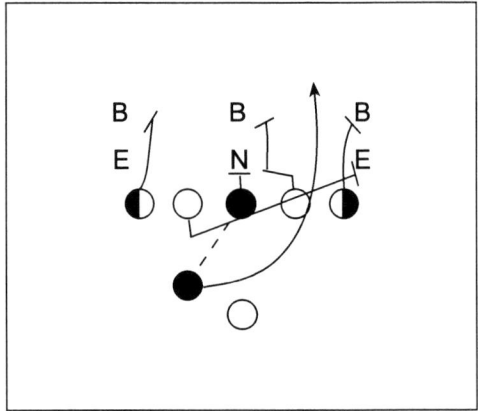

Figure 6-6d: Trap vs. 3-3

Player Responsibilities:

- FST—He should block down on first down lineman inside. If the gap is uncovered, he should go to the backside linebacker.
- FSG—He should pull and kick-out the first defender outside the box.
- C—He should block back on the first down lineman backside.
- BSG—He should pull and wrap around for the second linebacker in the box.
- BST—He should wall off or clear downfield for the safety of the backside hash defender.
- Blocking Back—He should set the edge and block down on first defender head-up to the outside frontside tackle.
- Slot Receiver—He should crack the first linebacker in the box.
- QB—He should carry out a boot fake to hold the backside defensive end.

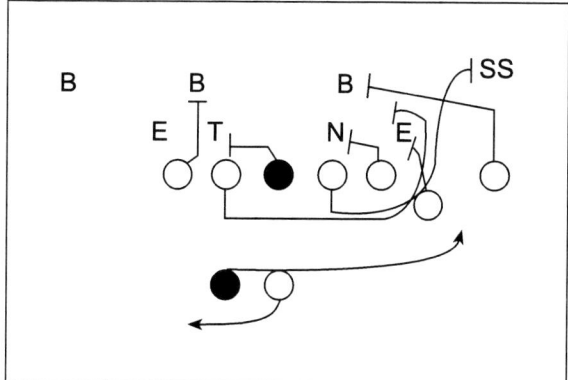

Figure 6-7: Sweep

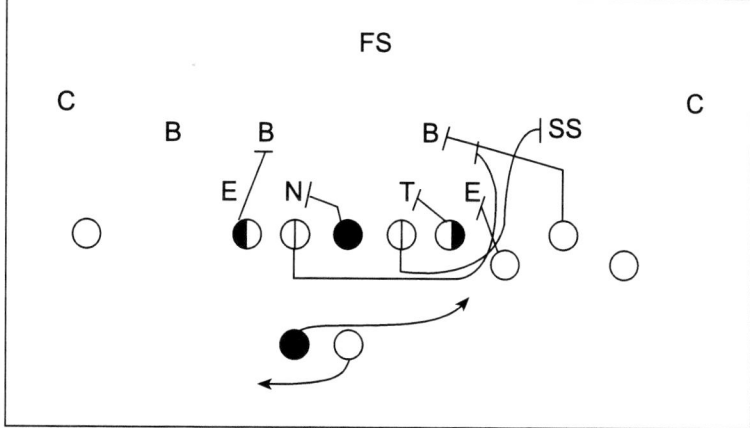

Figure 6-8a: Sweep vs. 4-2

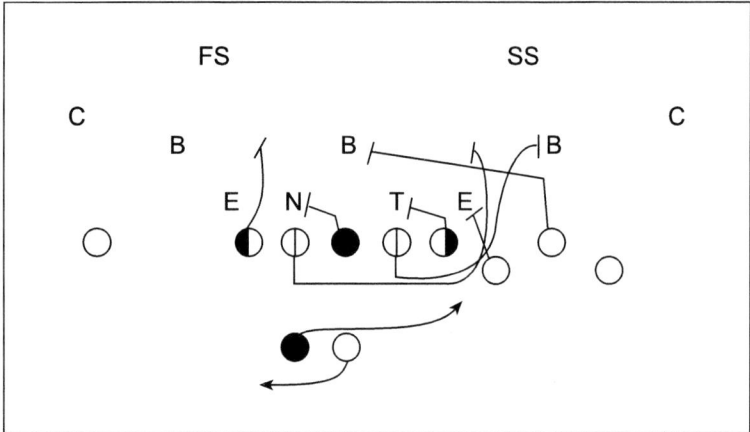

Figure 6-8b: Sweep vs. 4-1

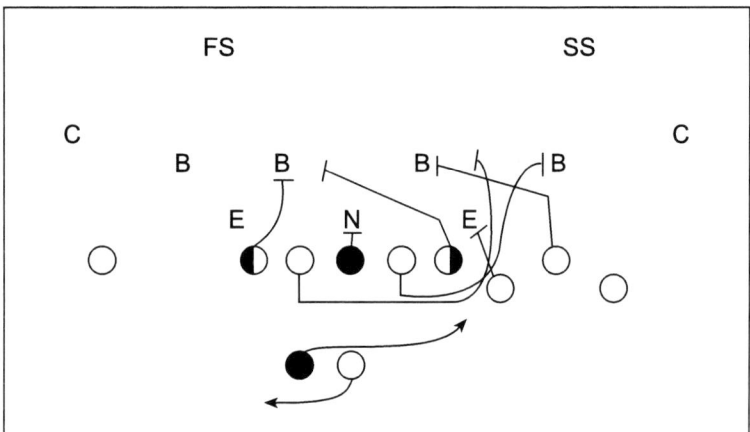

Figure 6-8c: Sweep vs. 3-2

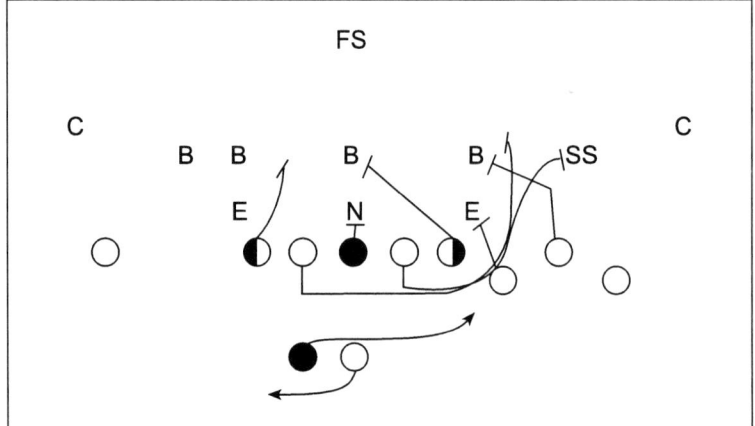

Figure 6-8d: Sweep vs. 3-3

Coaching Points:

- The running back must get north/south as soon as possible.
- The guards must keep their eyes on the defenders as they pull to adjust to the defenders' movements.

The Power

When implementing the power, your goal is to build a wall inside, kick out the edge, and wrap through for the frontside linebacker in the box. You should direct this play to the 1 technique or shade the noseguard to gain a free release by the frontside tackle to the backside linebacker. You should run this versus six in the box or less (Figures 6-9 and 6-10). The frontside keys in the power are as follows:

- If the inside gap is covered by a down lineman, he is basically the guard's and tackle's responsibility.
- If the inside gap is uncovered, the tackle will track to the backside linebacker.

Player Responsibilities:

- FST—He should double with the guard versus a 2 or 3 technique. If he is uncovered, he should track to the second linebacker in the box.
- FSG—He should double with the tackle versus a 2 or 3 technique. He should also be watching for the backside linebacker to run through.
- C—He should block back on the first down lineman backside.
- BSG—He should pull through the playside B gap for the frontside linebacker in the box.
- BST—He should pick-n-hinge with the center on the down lineman and come off on the edge defender late.
- Blocking Back—He should kick-out first thing head-up to the outside frontside tackle.
- QB—He should carry out a boot fake to hold the backside defensive end.

Coaching Points:

- You must establish movement on the double-team versus a 2 or 3 technique.
- The aiming point is from the frontside B gap to the frontside A gap.
- The backside guard must pull through the B gap. If no hole exists, he should make one.
- The backside tackle must provide body presence on the pick-n-hinge to close off the backside B gap.

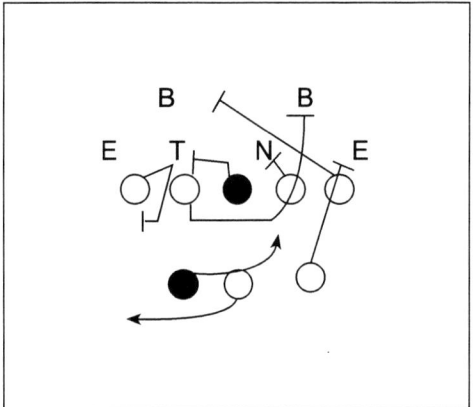

Figure 6-9: Power

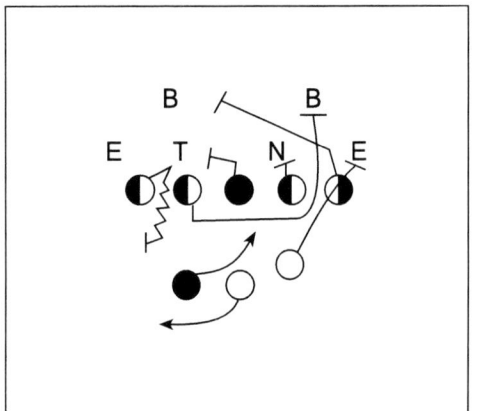

Figure 6-10a: Power vs. 4-2

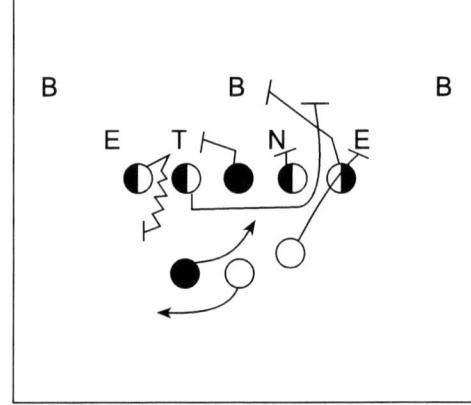

Figure 6-10b: Power vs. 4-1

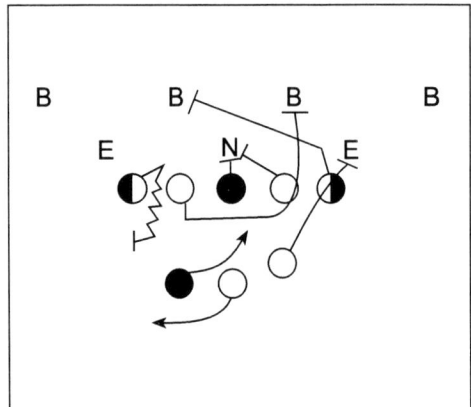

Figure 6-10c: Power vs. 3-2

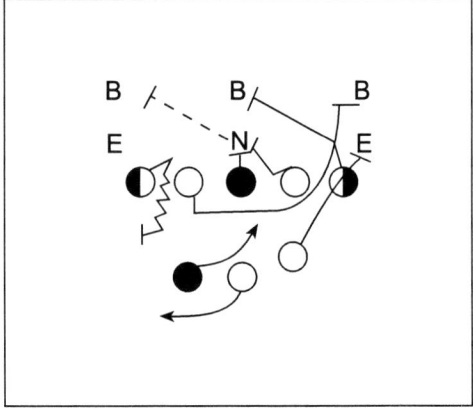

Figure 6-10d: Power vs. 3-3

72

CHAPTER 7

The Hurry-Up, No-Huddle Passing Game

This chapter illustrates four basic combination-passing routes in the hurry-up offense, including the alignments, player responsibilities, and coaching points for each route. The routes also include drills to help you develop your players' execution of each play.

The Smash

The *smash* route can be run versus any secondary coverage. It is also a very good complement to the four-verticals route if the outside linebackers are getting depth to try and stop the inside receivers from getting open upfield (Figure 7-1).

Alignments:

- Inside Receiver—He should move the outside linebacker in as far as possible, which creates an opening for the stop route by the outside receiver.
- Outside Receiver—His distance will be determined by the strength of your quarterback's arm. A good rule for an average armed quarterback is 10 to 12 yards from the tackle.

- One Back—He should align himself beside the quarterback and away from the play to stay out of the throwing lane, and to also keep the inside linebackers honest.

Player Responsibilities:

- Inside Receiver—After aligning properly, he should run a basic flag route over the top of the cornerback. His route should aim toward the back pylon of the end zone.
- Outside Receiver—After aligning properly, he should run a five-yard stop route turning to the inside and expecting the ball as soon as his turn is complete. After catching the ball, he should then turn to the sideline keeping the ball in his outside hand and away from the defenders.
- Quarterback—Prior to the snap, the quarterback should look to see if the defense is giving him the five-yard stop route. If the defense is vulnerable to the stop route, he should receive the snap without taking a drop and immediately throw to the outside receiver's hand nearest to the sideline. If the pre-snap read dictates the stop route will not be successful, the quarterback will take a three step drop from the shotgun and the read the cornerback to make a decision on who is open. Your rule for the quarterback is that if the cornerback takes more than a three-step backpedal, he must throw to the flat. A less than three-step backpedal by the cornerback and the quarterback should throw to the flag route over the top.

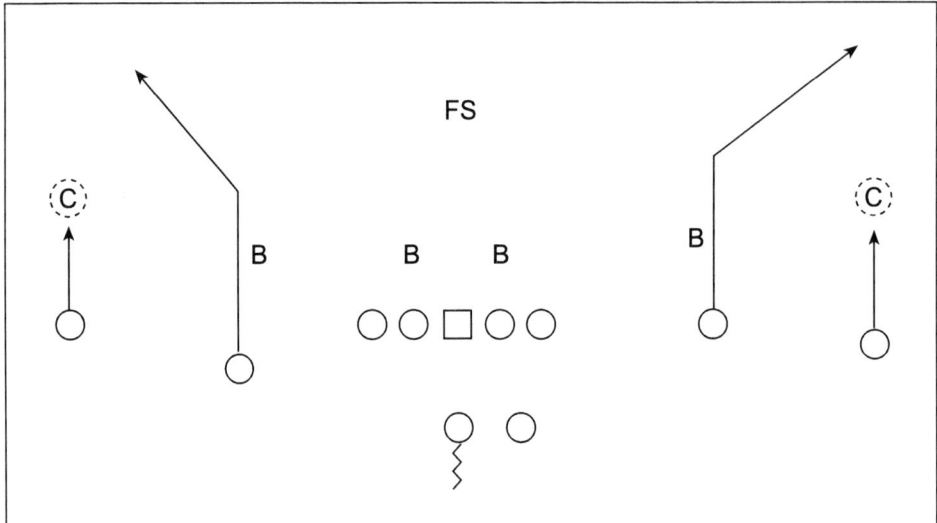

Figure 7-1

Adjustments Versus Two-Safety Coverages

The quarterback has the same read as in cover 3. If the cornerback takes short drop, the quarterback should throw to the flag. If the safety is over the top of the flag, the quarterback should throw to the progression of the stop route (Figure 7-2).

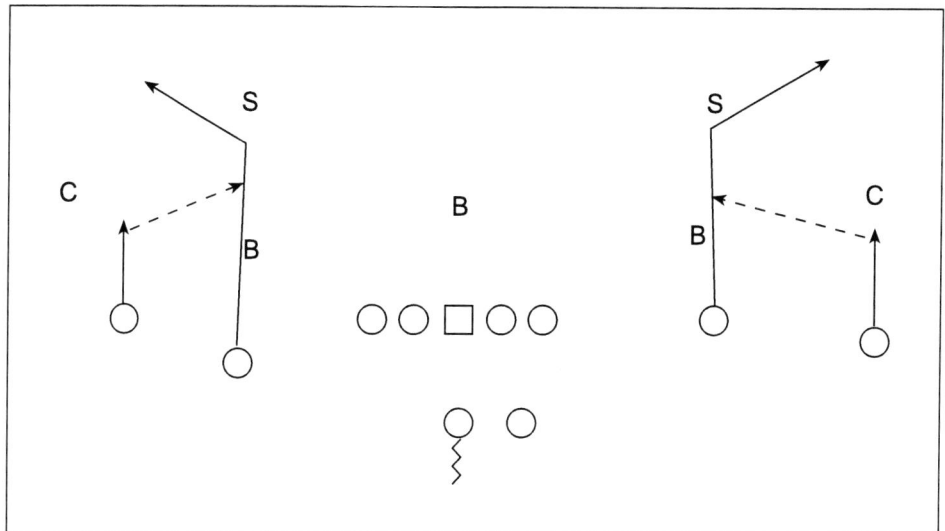

Figure 7-2

The Smash Drill

Have a stationary receiver five-yards downfield and 15 yards from the ball. As soon as the snap is received, the quarterback should slide his front foot and turn his front shoulder toward the receiver target releasing the ball as soon as possible. The coach's alignment should be 10 yards from the outside receiver and four or five yards off the line of scrimmage. When the ball is snapped, the coach should move quickly to imitate a linebacker getting under the stop route (Figure 7-3).

If the center-quarterback exchange has good timing and location, then the quarterback should be able to throw quick enough to complete the pass before the coach gets there. This will give the quarterback a good understanding of the route's possible success by the alignment of outside linebacker, and whether he can complete it in a game situation. The quarterback should throw at least 25 catchable balls to both sides two or three times a week during the off-season.

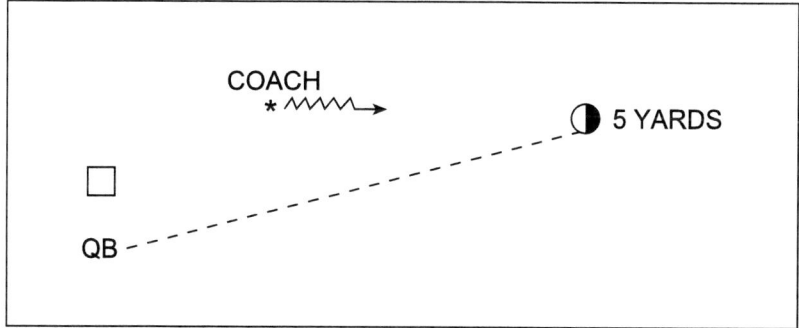

Figure 7-3

The Four Verticals

The four-verticals passing route in the hurry-up offense has the most big-play potential. It is used to stretch the defensive secondary, exploiting their weaknesses downfield. The route can be executed against any coverage with minor adjustments to the route and timing (Figure 7-4).

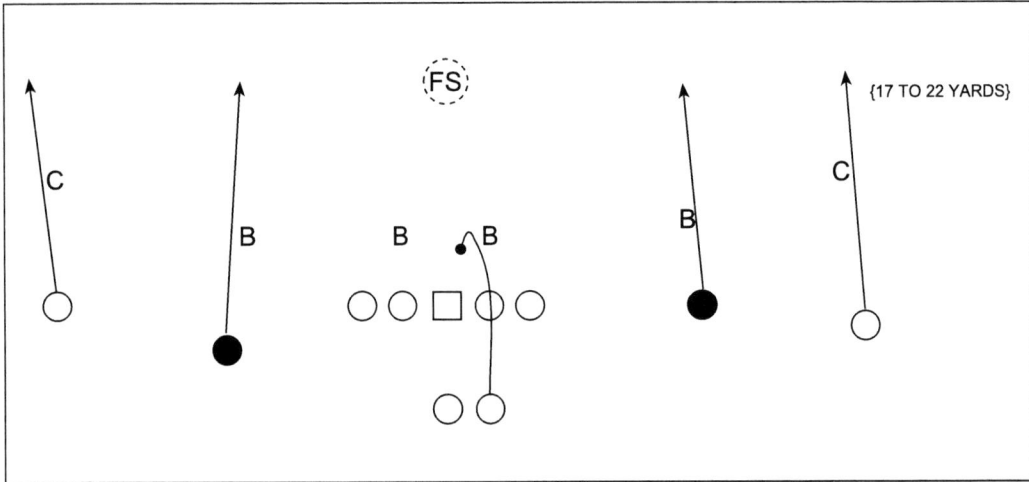

Figure 7-4

Alignments:

- Inside Receiver—He should split the difference between the outside receiver and the location of the ball.
- Outside Receiver—He should align himself as wide as the middle of the numbers.
- One Back—He should align himself next to the quarterback to keep the inside linebacker honest.

Player Responsibilities:

- Inside Receiver—After aligning properly, he should take an outside release getting off the line of scrimmage cleanly. All collisions with the outside linebacker should be avoided to keep the timing of the route and the spacing of the seams correct. Once the linebacker is cleared, the receiver should find the seam directly between the free safety and the cornerback and start looking for the ball over his inside shoulder. The quarterback should deliver the ball at a distance of 17 to 22 yards.
- Outside Receiver—He should occupy the cornerback by running full speed to his outside shoulder. This technique will keep him from becoming part of the play when thrown to the inside receiver. If the cornerback is playing tight zone or press

man, the outside receiver should adjust and run a five-yard stop route. This should also keep the cornerback from making a play on the inside receiver.

- Quarterback—After receiving the snap, the quarterback should take a three-step drop while keeping his eyes on the free safety. When his back foot lands upon completing his third step, he should throw to the appropriate receiver.

Coaching Points:

This is the first play you want to run versus a cover 3 secondary. If this play is executed properly, most teams will abandon the single-safety coverage. Your objective is to create a 2-on-1 situation between the free safety and your two inside receivers. This scenario is fulfilled if your outside receivers do their job of occupying the cornerbacks. It is the quarterback's responsibility to look off the free safety and throw back to the opposite receiver. His optimum distance to delivering the ball is 17 to 22 yards. This distance should be coached very specifically during practice so it becomes second nature. Another factor for the quarterback to consider after he has looked off the free safety is the drop of the inside linebacker to the playside. If the inside linebacker blitzes or is very focused on the running back in the backfield, the quarterback should be trained to get the ball to the receiver as soon as possible, usually within 17 yards. If the linebacker drops to a hook zone, the quarterback is responsible for putting the necessary trajectory on the ball to clear him, hence lengthening the route to about 22 yards. If it is thrown over 22 yards, a quality cornerback will make a play on the receiver. The running back in the backfield is responsible for picking up the blitz on the playside; if no one blitzes, the back runs a checkdown route in front of the playside linebacker at a depth of five yards. This route is used by the quarterback if the linebacker flies back deeper than 12 yards. This usually does not occur, but it is necessary to give the quarterback a release outlet.

Adjustments Versus Two-Safety Coverages

You should look to the widest playing safety while the playside receiver runs a nine-yard quick post inside him (Figure 7-5).

Player Responsibilities:

- Inside Receiver—(playside) He should run a nine-yard quick post with a head fake to the outside with a safety over the top.

    (backside) He should run the vertical route to the safety's outside shoulder.

- Outside Receiver—He should run a vertical route to occupy the cornerback.
- Quarterback—Instead of eyeing the free safety, he should freeze the middle linebacker with his eyes. After his three-step drop, he should deliver the ball to the receiver running the quick post at 12 to 15 yards. This should keep the backside

safety from getting involved. If the playside safety bites hard on the quick post, the quarterback should throw to the outside shoulder of the outside receiver on the same side.

- One Back—He must be responsible for blitz and pass protection. If no blitz occurs, he will run a five-yard checkdown route to occupy the middle linebacker and give the quarterback a release outlet.

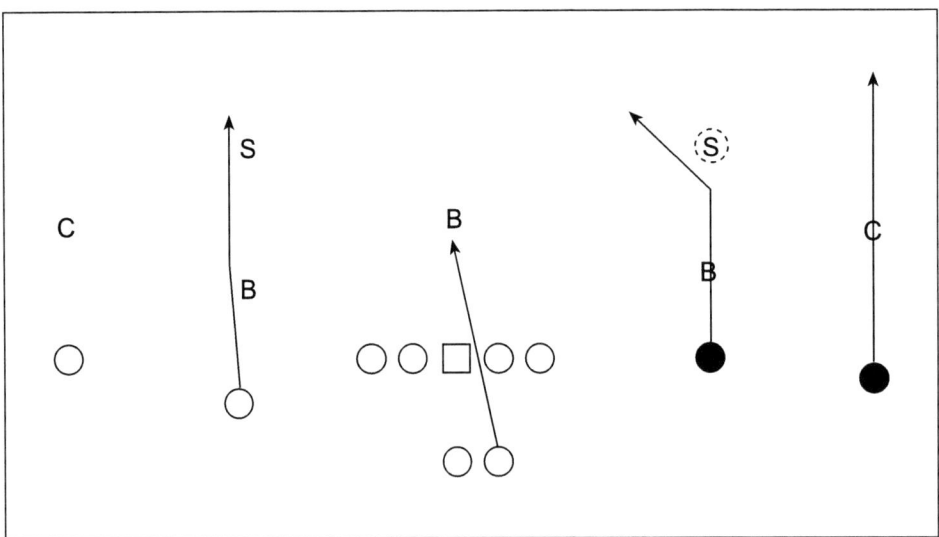

Figure 7-5

The Four-Verticals Drill

This is a very specific drill that you should use for the four verticals play. Put a receiver standing stationary, looking over his inside shoulder on the hash, 20 yards from the line of scrimmage. The #1 quarterback should be aligned in the middle of the field with the #2 quarterback snapping the ball. The coach should align 10 yards in a hook zone imitating a dropping linebacker. Once the ball is snapped, the #2 quarterback stands up to act as the eyes of the free safety, and the coach raises his hands to show the quarterback the height he must clear on the completion to the receiver (Figure 7-6). After each repetition, the #2 quarterback should tell the #1 quarterback if he looked the free safety off well enough.

Prior to the snap, the quarterback should look to see which side has the widest seam between the free safety and the cornerback. This will determine the side he throws to and his actions after receiving the snap. After receiving the snap, the quarterback should take a three-step drop from the shotgun formation, getting to a depth of about eight yards. While taking the drop, he will look over the opposite shoulder of the free safety. This will allow the quarterback to use his peripheral vision to the playside to keep an eye on the underneath coverage. He doesn't have to make the free safety move opposite, but just keep him in the middle of the field. On the last step, the quarterback should plant and look playside at the same time and release the ball to his intended receiver. The quarterback should learn to throw at least 25 catchable balls to each side three times a week during the off-season. During the season this drill needs to be executed twice a week with the inside receivers actually running the route.

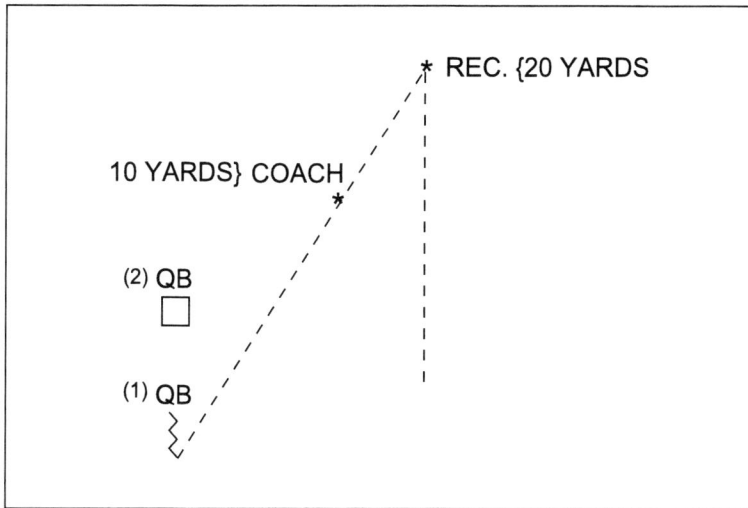

Figure 7-6

The Arrow

The *arrow* route is the hurry-up route that gives defenses the most trouble to defend in short-yardage situations. This route can also be run against any defense. Most teams implementing the arrow run it with the inside receiver and complement it with the outside receiver on a curl route. The hurry-up offense uses a quick slant by the outside receiver as the equalizer to the arrow because the pass protection is easier and the receiver catches the ball on the run (Figure 7-7).

Alignments:

- Inside Receiver—He should be positioned five yards from the offensive tackle. Any wider than this and the throw from the quarterback becomes difficult due to a bad angle.
- Outside Receiver—He should be 10 yards from the inside receiver, or not any wider than the bottom of the numbers. This distance creates a good seam for the quarterback and allocates time for the outside linebacker to be read.

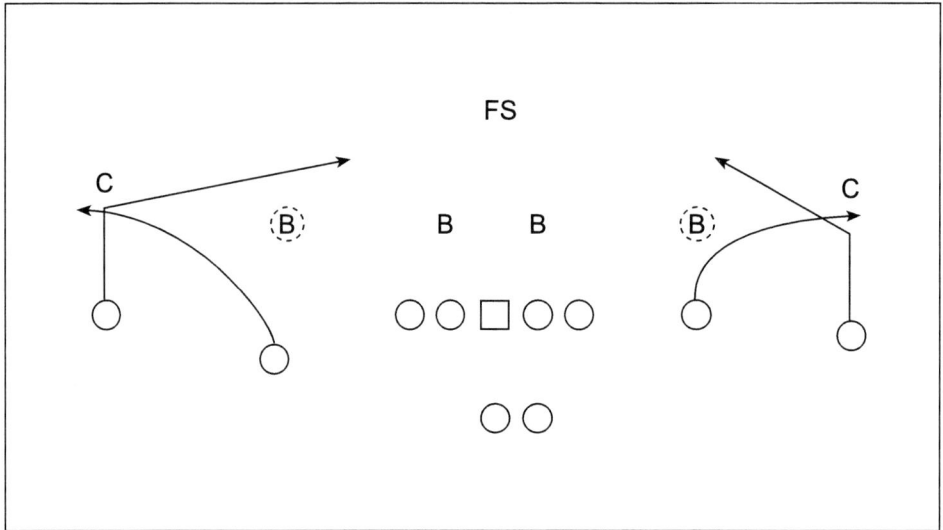

Figure 7-7

- One Back—He should align himself next to the quarterback, but away from the throwing side to keep the throwing lane open.

Player Responsibilities:

- Inside Receiver—After aligning properly, he should run a five-yard speed route without making a cut. He should round off the route and look for the ball over his outside shoulder.

- Outside Receiver— After aligning properly, he should run a four-yard quick slant. After the head fake, the route should be at a 45-degree angle behind the outside linebacker. He should expect the ball once he clears the outside linebacker.

- Quarterback—Due to the nature of the route, the he should take the snap and make an immediate read on the outside linebacker. He should not dropback. He should deliver the ball to the proper receiver.

Coaching Points:

The quarterback read is based on the outside linebacker. If the outside linebacker drops straight back, the quarterback immediately throws to the arrow. If the outside linebacker drops at a 45-degree angle, the quarterback should throw to the quick slant. The timing on the quick slant is triggered when the receiver gets directly behind the outside linebacker. The ball has to be released to a spot just ahead of the receiver in between the inside and outside linebackers.

When the quarterback throws to the speed out, he should never throw behind the receiver. If it is a bad throw, it must be to the outside. When throwing to the quick slant, the throw must be between the numbers and the belt. Anything higher has a good chance of being intercepted if not handled cleanly by the receiver. After the quarterback understands this play, he can look at the inside linebacker while using his peripheral vision to read outside linebacker. This will create a bigger seam for the quick slant.

Adjustments versus Two-Safety Coverages

You should look to the widest outside linebacker and the quarterback should be thinking slant (Figure 7-8).

Player Responsibilities:

- Inside Receiver—He should widen his alignment as wide as the outside linebacker will go. This will create a bigger seam for the quick slant.
- Outside Receiver—He should align six yards from the inside receiver. This allows the route to develop quicker.
- Quarterback—He will automatically throw the quick slant based on the standard two-safety coverage rules, especially if the opponent mixes in some cover 2. He should not take a chance on the cornerback playing a hard cover 2 and intercepting the ball. The quarterback must freeze the middle linebacker as long as possible creating a larger seam for the quick slant.

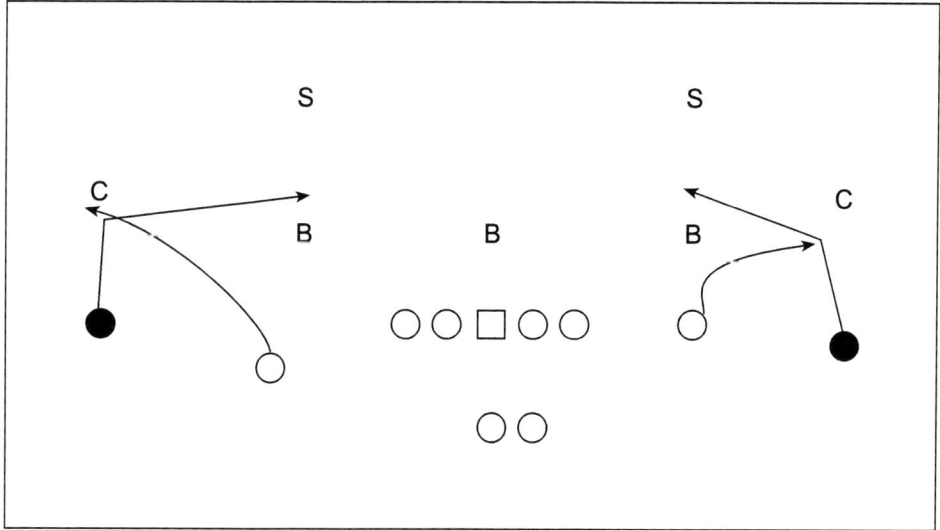

Figure 7-8

The Arrow Drill

Have your inside and outside receivers align properly with the coach being the outside linebacker. After the snap, the quarterback will read the coach whether he drops at a

45-degree angle or straight back. The quarterback's front foot should hesitate in case he has to throw the quick slant. It is easier to move toward the arrow-route late than have to bring the front foot back to the middle (Figure 7-9). The quarterback should throw at least 25 catchable balls to receivers on both sides two or three times a week in the off-season.

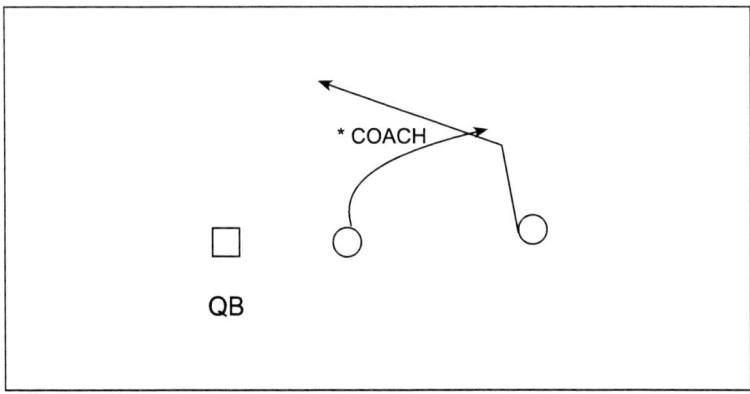

Figure 7-9

The Crossing

This is one of the main plays of the hurry-up offense when facing man coverage. Finding a matchup to your advantage, the target receiver will be rubbed off other crossing receivers. This creates separation between the receiver and defender making an easier throw for the quarterback.

Alignments:

- Slot Receiver (target)—He should align no further than four yards from offensive tackle. This allows the receiver to get across the field quicker.
- Slot Receiver (clear out)—He should align three yards from tackle.
- Playside Receiver—He should align two steps closer than normal, but without tipping the defense off to a change in alignment.

Player Responsibilities:

- Slot Receiver (target)—He should push his defender upfield three yards, make a head and shoulder fake outward, and then cut across the field. On the crossing route, he should find the opposite slot receiver and rub off of him. Once he clears the slot receiver, he should gradually get more depth, approximately six yards, looking for the ball as soon as he clears the offensive line box.

- Slot Receiver (clear out)—He should push upfield two yards, head fake, find the first inside linebacker to his side, and run right in front of him expecting to get hit. The inside linebacker can't knock him off course and into the target receiver. This is not a pick; it is a rub off, which is completely legal.
- Playside Receiver—He is the most important part of this play for it to be successful. He should take an outside release on his defender, keeping him from getting a visual on the crossing route. After getting his defender's back turned, he should gradually get across the field and not look up until crossing the middle. This will open the sideline up for the target receiver after he catches the ball.
- Quarterback—After taking the snap, he should take a three-step drop, looking straight downfield. He will pump fake opposite the play and will not focus on target receiver. Once the target receiver clears, he will deliver the ball 6- to 10-yards downfield.

Coaching Point:

You must find the best matchups based on the defense's personnel. The main coaching point is that the clear out receiver should get his defender's backs turned and out of the play. The quarterback may also have to move around in the pocket to buy some extra time and by getting more depth due to the defensive tendency to blitz while playing man coverage.

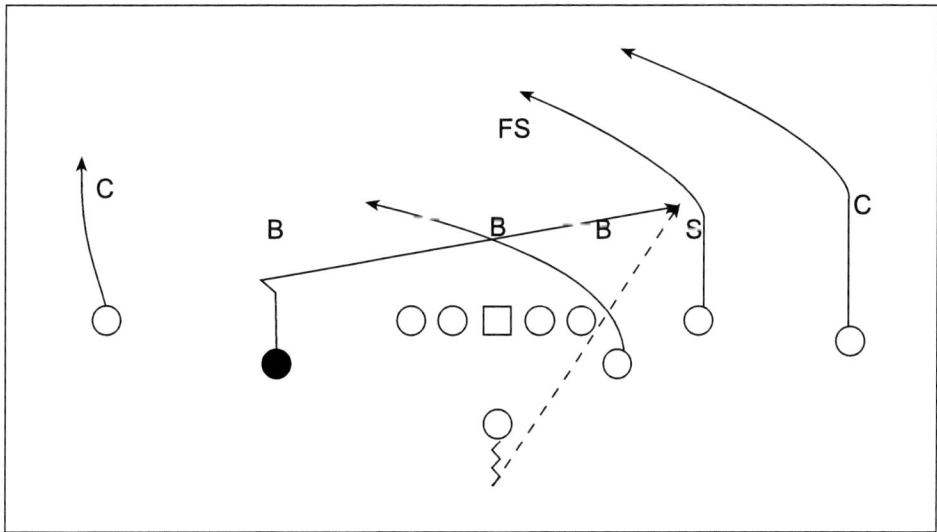

Figure 7-10

CHAPTER 8

Tips for Running the Hurry-Up, No-Huddle

After integrating the hurry-up, no-huddle system into your offense, the biggest factor in determining what success level your program achieves will be the attention and repetition you apply in practice. The following are 14 detailed tips that will help your staff and team achieve your goals for success:

- You should limit the number of plays and formations you teach at first. It is a good idea to give your players and coaches as little to memorize as possible when implementing the hurry-up, no-huddle. You want this to be a positive experience for your team and to give them the confidence they need to do this. The first time you implement this in practice, you should only used two or three plays and one formation, and then slowly add other formations and plays at a pace that both players and coaches can handle. Your goal should be to have your entire hurry-up offense ready by the end of the first week.

- You should limit the number of players that participate on both offense and defense, if at all possible. This really depends on the classification of your school. If your opponents play several players both ways, then it's all right for you to do the same. But if your opponents' players are one-way players, then you need to take this into account with your own. Usually your players will be able to play full-time on one side of the ball and half of the time on the other side without any problems.

- You should limit changes in the snap count. Give your athletes as little to think about as possible. You should only have one snap count that you use regularly. This will keep the pace of the game at the speed you want. You should not care if the defense knows your snap count, and you want them to get into a rhythm with it. That way, every fourth or fifth play you should run a dummy/dummy play to get the defense to jump offsides, or show you their coverage and blitzes, allowing you to audible to the correct play.

- You should notify your chain crew of their importance. You might notice the funny reaction you get the first time you talk to them about how important it is for them to be in good shape. They need to be able to move the chains as quickly as possible, and also be able to set in the proper position before the referee spots the ball. This allows the game to keep moving at a fast pace. When you are on the road in your pregame meeting with the officials, you need to address the issue of the visiting chain crew slow playing you. A slow chain crew can be devastating to the hurry-up philosophy.

- You should talk to the officials before each game. One of the first questions you should ask them in a pregame meeting is: Will the clock start when the box is set? This is an important factor in maintaining the pace of your offense. Bring it to the officials' attention that most white hats will start the clock when the box is set, and will not wait for the chains to be in place. After you start having some success at the hurry-up pace, opposing coaches will put pressure on the officials to slow the game down. Address the issue by reminding them the rule states that officials should officiate at the pace of the game. Let them know that your pace will be extremely fast. Tell them that you do not expect them to speed the game up, but to be sure to not slow it down. You should also ask the officials if you could run a new ball in on every single play, even if the weather is good. Every timesaving advantage will help.

- You should have your players hand the ball to the referee for two reasons. First, it is good sportsmanship, and if you don't think officials notice this, then ask them sometime; they do. Second, it keeps the game going at a faster pace because it takes valuable time for officials to retrieve discarded balls. You not only want to give the ball to the referee, but ideally to the umpire since he is the one that actually spots the location of the ball for the next play. If you have a player who does not hand the ball to an official, then make him do extra work in practice to help him understand the importance of this simple act.

- You should make sure your receivers do not retrieve incomplete passes. You have ball boys assigned to this job. The only thing they need to worry about is returning to the line of scrimmage as soon as possible and getting ready for the next play.

- You should have at least two dependable ball boys. Use two of your more dependable freshman players instead of your coach's young sons. This is an extremely important job. So important that you should put one of your coaches in charge of both ball boys. One ball boy should be responsible for retrieving incomplete passes, while the other should run a new ball into the umpire as soon as the previous play ends. Even if its not an incomplete pass, your ball boy can still run a new ball into the umpire to help speed up the pace of the game. Your ball boys will get a good workout during the course of a game. You should tell them they are just as important as any player on the field.

- You should not huddle during 7-on-7 games. This programs your quarterback and receivers to think quickly and gets them in game shape even before the season starts. It also programs your coaches to think quickly by calling the plays. This is actually more important for your coaches than for your players. It is easy for the athletes to run the hurry-up; the challenge is for the offensive coaches. Anything that gives them practice for a game situation will help them develop this ability.

- You should always have plenty of footballs available for games, bringing at least 20 footballs with you. You cannot afford to be waiting on footballs to run the offense even if weather conditions are not favorable.

- You should limit the use of motion in your offense whenever possible. This will help achieve the goal of snapping the ball within five seconds after the referee puts the ball in place.

- You should always practice at a faster pace than an actual game. You want the games to seem slow to your players and it help you execute your offense at a high level of effectiveness.

- You should practice these tips during every practice. It is just like anything else you do; the more you practice, the better you will be at it. Integrate the hurry-up, no-huddle philosophy into your entire practice schedule (see Chapter 5).

YEARLY OFFENSIVE GOAL CHART

	350 + TOTAL OFFENSIVE YARDS	60 + TOTAL PLAYS RUN	30 + POINTS SCORED	1 OR LESS TURNOVERS
Game 1				
Game 2				
Game 3				
Game 4				
Game 5				
Game 6				
Game 7				
Game 8				
Game 9				
Game 10				
Game 11				
Game 12				
Game 13				
Game 14				

Figure 8-1

ABOUT THE AUTHOR

Gus Malzahn is the head coach at Springdale High School, which is one of the tradition-rich programs in the state of Arkansas. In his first season at Springdale, his 2001 Bulldogs broke 12 offensive school records, and in 2002 he led them to the state championship game.

Malzahn began his coaching career in 1991 at Hughes High School as the defensive coordinator. The following season he was named to the head coaching position, which he held until 1995. In 1994, he led the Blue Devils to the state finals, which had been their only appearance in school history.

In 1996, he took the head coaching job at Shiloh Christian High School in Springdale, Arkansas. His compiled record at Shiloh was 63-7-1. In 1997, he implemented the hurry-up, no-huddle philosophy into his offense. For the next four years, the Shiloh offense was one of the nation's top yardage producers, averaging almost 7,000 yards per season. During his tenure at Shiloh, he led them to four state title appearances and two state championships. He also had two different quarterbacks who each set two national records. In 2000, his team was ranked as high as number 11 in the ESPN.com National High School Football rankings.

In the high school and college ranks, Gus Malzahn is often called on to speak to coaching staffs about his hurry-up, no-huddle offense. He also speaks several times a year at clinics around the country.